THE FREEWOOD
YEARS

THE
FREEWOOD
YEARS

Mary Denyer

Michael O'Mara Books Limited

First published in Great Britain in 1998 by
Michael O'Mara Books Limited
9 Lion Yard, Tremadoc Road
London SW4 7NQ

A CIP catalogue record for this book
is available from the British Library.

ISBN 1-85479-389-6

1 3 5 7 9 10 8 6 4 2

Designed and typeset by
The Florence Group, Stoodleigh, Devon

Printed and bound by WSOY, Finland

CONTENTS

PUBLISHER'S FOREWORD

DURING the Second World War, Mary Denyer (then Mrs Savidge) and her young son John went to live in a small thatched cottage in Freewood, Suffolk. With her husband away at war, her eldest son doing National Service and her daughter at drama school, Mary and John immersed themselves in a world of their own, caring for the wildlife of the wood. Their cottage soon became home to a succession of 'uninvited guests' – wounded or orphaned animals and birds. Written during that time, Mary later put her manuscript in a drawer and forgot all about it until her elder son, Ivan, discovered it recently. Mary Denyer is now ninety-five years old, twice-widowed, and living in Pembrokeshire and it is only now that she realises how others might wish to share the enchantment of Freewood and its animals as she captured it so long ago. At her request, her manuscript remains as she wrote it, a

personal piece of history charmingly augmented
by the illustrations John drew of the animals at the
time.

INTRODUCTION

I MIGHT have called this book *Uninvited*, because
the guests who came were like that: they arrived
in the most unexpected ways. We have lived in
rather isolated places and become absorbed with
interest in the creatures we have found around us.
They brought their own compensation, and out of
all the birds and beasts we cared for, only one
refused its friendship.

John found it on the roadside, a turtledove,
missing every tail feather. It was at the end of the
summer, and its fellows had taken flight. We knew
that if it were left it would either die of starvation
or be killed, so he brought it indoors and put it in
a large cage. In this it had plenty of room to walk
about and stretch its wings.

A small boy's pocket-money was slender, and
grain and seed dear enough, but young John had
made this his pigeon, so to say, and though it ate
an enormous amount it was sufficiently wasteful to
leave ample for the canaries. He kept it through
the winter, until it had grown a full set of tail

feathers, and the weather was mild enough to let it go. It never showed the smallest interest in our advances, though it shared the kitchen. It was neither nervous nor afraid, but it had no more character than a clockwork doll. It even made no sound except when pecking seed. When John took its cage outside and opened the door, this impersonal little ruffian flew straight up into an oak tree, rested a moment, and flew out of sight without so much as a glance.

As I write, there are two red-legged partridges precisely stepping on the lawn outside this window. They flick their tails with each step, and are making a clucking sound, almost like the ticking of a grandfather clock. They are nervously alert, watching and listening for the slightest alarm, which will send them running into the tall dry grass. They take a daily dust-bath in our garden at all times of the year. The soil near the south wall is dry and fine, overhung by a thatch so deep that rain rarely soaks the ground beneath it. I opened the door a few days ago, not knowing that they were there, and a covey of them went up, leaving a cloud of dust.

A pheasant is strutting down one of the rides, safe now that the 'season' is closed. He pauses to raise his proud head, *ko-chok*s, with an accompanying flurry and clatter of his wings, and struts on. He reminds me of one we knew: we were walking in the woods one day and put up a hen pheasant, who, instead of taking to the air, limped hurriedly into the bracken, falling as she went. John followed her, knowing she must be injured, and found that one foot had been shattered in a rabbit-gin. We carried her home, washed, disinfected, and bound her leg, and put her into the empty squirrel house, covering the floor with a deep layer of loose dried bracken for her to hide in. She crouched, burying her head in the fronds. We left her a bowl of water and threw grain into the bracken. Although we thought we might have to kill her, we wanted to give her a chance.

We left her alone, apart from checking to see that she was feeding and drinking. She did not peck her bandage and, except for a lowering of the head, she did not panic when we touched her. We kept her for a week, and by that time she had learned to walk quite well, though lame. So we carried her to where we had found her, and let her go. We never saw her again, once she had vanished into the undergrowth, but these woods are vast, and she had every chance of surviving unless she met a fox. We knew she would never be shot, because a man does not shoot a bird (in Britain) unless it is on the wing and, perhaps due to extended injury, she could not fly.

Jays are screeching in the hazel trees that edge the clearing beyond the garden. Not very many are shot; they are too wary, darting away before a man can raise his gun, but they are treated as

vermin by gamekeepers, and many a clutch is destroyed by a shot through the nest at breeding time. We decided to save a fledgeling for a friend of ours who had a large outdoor aviary inhabited by many wild birds.

We had had no experience of jays before, and felt that we should rear only one at a time. We prepared a parrot cage, with branches across the interior at varying heights and a rough nest on the floor. From the first moment of his entry, he was at home and took the centre of the stage. He hopped about, raised his crest, screeched, and sorted over the straw with his beak. John pushed the usual mixture into his mouth (chopped egg, insects, cereal and milk), and he soon *chark*-ed for more. His cage hung in the kitchen where there was light and warmth, and where he could see human beings constantly. He heard the plop-plop of the drops of water which fell from the leaky tap over the sink, and weeks afterwards in his aviary he made this sound so accurately that one could not have told the difference between the tap and the jay. It was startlingly exact.

We never set out to teach Jay to talk. He taught himself. 'Hullo, Mummy' and 'Goodbye' were his first choice. He was a friendly bird; he would watch our faces and raise his crest, bending his head from left to right while he listened intently. Then he would wipe his beak on the perch and think about what he'd heard. The repetition of it for the first time was always to himself as he hopped about his cage. While he was with us, our Siamese cat had a litter of kittens who, because they explored cupboards, larder, flour-bin, holes and corners, often caused me to ask: 'Where are the cats?' So it was really very funny when one day as I entered the kitchen Jay asked: 'Where are the cats?' before I had had time to look. It was a quite uncannily accurate imitation.

When he was full-grown we took him away to the prepared aviary. He was pleasantly friendly towards the other birds, and soon mystified a Sealyham bitch by mimicking her bark: she would run, and stop, and wait with ears cocked, quite baffled.

One memory calls up another, as when I watch red squirrels from this window, playing together, bounding up a tree trunk, jumping from branch to branch, hanging from the slenderest twigs in their passage from one bough to another. At once I am reminded of the squirrels John caught and failed to tame and carried into the woods again, seeing them skip up the straight trunk of the pine tree, to turn and lash their tails and swear at us – '*skobble-skobble*' – and bound away again, only to peep at us from behind a branch, and continue to run and peep until we had gone and left them.

The pine tree: looking up I can see the dome of blue above it, and the willow tree outlined against the blue in a thick, overgrown copse bearing on the top branch a nightingale. It was Easter Sunday morning, the 5th of April, the earliest date recorded for their arrival in Freewood. I was cooking, when suddenly the door opened and John said: 'Come quickly, but be very quiet. The nightingale's here, and he's singing on a branch. I can see him and all his body is quivering.' John and his sister and I walked, very slowly and without speaking or looking up, until we were underneath the branch where the nightingale was pouring his song through the pausing air. We watched him, enchanted, for minutes, his throat vibrating, his whole self indifferent to our presence. He was so slender, and he cocked his tail as a wren does. He was still singing when we walked away – he had shown no interest in our coming or going. We have seen them on the ground fighting for territory, and we once built a hide to observe them, but we never saw a nest in all our months of trying.

Everywhere I look I am reminded of some incident which happened unasked. Not all of them were successful, however. We were given some goldfish, and they thrived so well in the aquarium that we transferred them to a small pond in the corner of our garden, hoping they would breed. We visited them every morning, but one day there was not one to be seen. We stirred the water and searched the weeds. No trace: had wild duck been flying over and seen them? The odds were against it. We did not have to wonder long. Early one morning we saw a heron drinking there, and as he rose over the meadow and flapped lazily on his way, we knew.

Then two newts occupied the aquarium, with several water-snails. They had a wooden raft floating in it, where the newts could lie and sun themselves. They flourished for a summer, and

the male grew into a handsome specimen. Imagine how surprised we were one morning to find that during the night they had vanished. No heron this time, and no cats. The unsolved mystery made us believe that they had crawled out and somehow reached the outdoors to hibernate under a stone or log. Frogs and toads travel considerable distances for this, and we had to conclude that the newts had done the same; after all, it was only a few yards to the nearest door.

Obviously our luck lay not in aquatic circles but with birds and animals. Except for the greenfinches: John found a partly destroyed nest of four half-fledged young ones. He picked it up and reassembled it as well as he could in a wooden box, replacing the young birds, and setting the whole thing on its side in a hedge, with wire netting over the front to keep them safe from further attack or from falling. Then he hid until he had seen the parent feeding them through the wire.

It worked splendidly, and the young ones grew and moved about the box trying their small strength. One morning, when they were almost due for release, John found one dead, with its throat and breast bleeding. The next morning he went early, and found another in a similar condition. He removed it, and hid himself, determined to catch the rat or rook unawares. He watched the parent bird fly to the box and the two babies rush to the wire with open beaks. She pushed food into one mouth, and then remained at the wire for some time. John spent most of the day watching, but only the greenfinch visited the box. After a long visit by the parent he went to look, and found that one small bird had a blood mark on its throat, a fresh one. He came home distressed and puzzled; and we decided that the parent bird had killed them, trying to get them out of the nest, she having felt it time that they were flying. A bird has no intelligence, only natural reactions. John removed the wire and loosed the one remaining fledgeling, and sure enough, the adult bird flew down and continued feeding it, ignoring the nest.

In 'Mallard and Co.', I talk about 'Nutkin' Squirrel, our old farmer friend. I must tell here what there was no place for in that chapter: he was around seventy-five years old, and as a child had lived in the farmhouse we were occupying. We heard of him when we first came south, and that it was his father who had planted the great lime tree that grew on the lawn outside the sitting-room window, and which cast a parasol of shade in summer (when it was in flower it filled the house with its sweet scent, and wore a veritable shawl of bees). So I asked him to lunch with us. He came, and delighted in his old haunts. He wandered everywhere, downstairs, upstairs, in the outhouses, stables, garden. He remembered every corner and discovered many alterations.

We had our meal, and sat on while he smoked a cigarette and reminisced. As we moved from the table I saw him walk straight towards the wall beside the dining-room window and suddenly stop and turn to me. 'Good gracious! Do you know what I just did? We had a barometer hanging here, and I went to look at it as I always did when I was a lad.' He seemed quite moved by this lapse into the past, as well he might, momentarily having bridged sixty years.

Today, there is a green woodpecker on the grass outside the window. He is digging for ants with his strong beak, and when he finds their nest, his long tongue will explore it deep down and supply him with a rare feed. The sun covers him with gold-dust and heightens the scarlet of his cap. If he sees me watching him he will dart into the cover of the woods with *a wip-wip-wip* of alarm . . . as even now he is doing. But to my stories: they are true accounts of the strangest guests we had. Do not, in your minds, endow wild creatures with human intelligence. They act, and react, and are governed by animal law. They have no understanding, no knowledge of death or suffering; but they know fear, and hunger, and thirst, and feel pain. They have a right to our care and consideration. They are in any event at our mercy. I have heard so often: 'But nature itself is cruel; look what animals do to each other.' There is only one reply: 'We are not animals.'

CAPTAIN CUTTLE
RFJ

YOU ASK 'What does RFJ mean?' It means
Royal Flight of Jackdaws. This is the story of
one of its illustrious members.

An old elm tree stood at the corner of the stack-
yard, and, about twelve feet from the ground, a
hole as big as a child's bath had for several springs
housed families of jackdaws. Immense business
could be heard from earliest light until dusk.
This particular year, sticks and rubbish of various
kinds had been flown into the hole, and there had
been much talking and deliberating on the higher
branches. Preening was mixed with jabbering and
strutting on stacks and trees. Later, the male bird
would enter his apartment with loaded beak, stay
a moment, and fly away again, seeking further
offerings. Then things had become quieter.

This, we felt, must mean a sitting of eggs, and
we got a ladder and climbed up to see. Sure
enough, there were four eggs low down in the

dark hollow. The nest was of sticks, strands of sheep-wool, and dried grass mixed with bits of paper and wood. While we examined it the parent birds were confused and angry, and immediately the ladder was removed one of them flew in.

For more than two weeks the female sat on the eggs, while the male brought food to her. Once the eggs were hatched we left them alone for three weeks, but at the end of that time we took one of the young ones to rear. Many daws are shot every year on account of the damage they do, and so turning one into a pet seemed a good idea.

We prepared a box about a cubic foot in size, with straw on the bottom and a piece of wire netting on the top. We stood it on the window-ledge in the dining-room, and went to fetch him. He was extremely ugly and smelt a trifle sour. An enormous beak edged with bright yellow skin seemed disproportionately large compared with his head. His cheeks were not fully feathered. He had several bald patches, and his wing feathers were still 'wrapped'. He flattened his crest and cringed each time anyone approached, but he had shuffled down into the straw and was fat and warm. We chopped hard-boiled egg with brown bread and milk, insects, small worms and spiders, and for the first two feeds had to open his beak with a matchstick, and push the mush down his throat with a twisted 'spoon' we had improvised out of fluffy pipe-cleaners. After that, his beak flew wide open whenever one of us passed the box.

He soon began to preen and free his feathers of their casings. He ceased to cringe, and in a few days was standing up and wafting his wings with excitement at feeding time, which was almost continuous from seven in the morning until we retired to bed.

The wire netting had been removed shortly after he arrived, to give him freedom of movement. One day, while we were having lunch, he was standing on the side of his box wafting his wings when he suddenly found himself airborne. The next stop was the middle of the polished table, where he slithered and slid and tried to reach a dish, calling '*chack*'. Obviously something had to be done. So, later, we fixed a scraped branch at right angles to the wall in the kitchen (where there was a stone floor and a scrubbed table), and made it his perch. The dining-room became out of bounds.

There was a brick wall surrounding the yard outside the kitchen door. As he grew our daw spent most of his time patrolling this, and jabbering in what we thought must be a secret language. We named him Captain Cuttle, but called him Cappy for short. He came when we called him, and if he were not in sight I would clap my hands and he would appear at once, chattering and settling on me. He loved a ride on our shoulders, and would go anywhere in that position, even for a drive in the car.

One day when he was a few months old, I was cutting the lawn edges with shears, and Cappy was by my side catching insects. Quite unexpectedly he jumped on to the blades as I snipped, and the longest toe of his right foot lost its end. It dripped with blood and I hurried him indoors, washed it with antiseptic, and bandaged it. Then I put him in a box of hay and made him rest for a few hours by keeping him in the dark.

When I eventually went to look at him, he had pecked off the bandage and was in a fine old mess. It looked as if he might bleed to death unless something could be done to stanch it. I therefore slung him in a large kerchief so that he could not move his wings or reach his feet, but had his head free to see and feed. At the end of three days he was

healed and loosed. That foot was our means of identifying him later in his career, after he had been away for several weeks flying wild.

We taught him many words, without slitting his tongue, which is unnecessary and most cruel. He would call 'John, John,' repeating it for minutes on end while walking along his wall, and then remark: 'Right!' 'Hullo Jack' was another phrase he liked, and he would mimic my 'Oh!' at the most amusing moments.

He loved his kitchen perch and slept there standing on one leg with his head tucked round and hidden in his back feathers. When awake he always looked busy, strutting about, nibbling things with the tip of his beak, then wiping that beak from side to side on the nearest object – which, if it happened to be one's neck, was a mixed pleasure. He kept himself very clean and well groomed, spending much time on his appearance. He loved a bowl of water to bathe in; and when the sun was warm, he would crouch in the grass, rolling to one side, stretching the far wing as high into the air as he could, his head feathers raised and his visible eye wide open, staring upward. Then the other side would be sunned in the same way. This, I discovered, is called 'anting'. The first time Cappy did this, John, then quite young, rushed to fetch me – 'Come quickly, there is something the matter with Cappy. I think he is dying.'

Our bull-terrier, Game, quite used to the occasional arrival of some odd creature or other, took no notice of Cappy once we had allowed her to take a very comprehensive sniff of him. But as time went on, Captain Cuttle became rather a handful in many ways. An open window was irresistible to him, and one day he appeared at the back door with lipstick on his face, holding the capless stick in one foot. He flew on to my shoulder, and wiped his red beak on a new cardigan I was wearing. After three lipsticks had disappeared, and several other oddments from dressing-tables, we decided we had to keep the windows closed – not ideal in summer!

He had the most lovable way of standing sleek, with wings folded, and bowing his head. I rubbed the tip of my nose into the nape of his neck, and he would make a little murmur, a muffled *jack-jack-jack*, showing his delight. Bowing the head in this way shows complete confidence. We loved him dearly, but he caused a good deal of work.

When the wild daws flew over he cocked one eye up at them, and his wings moved slowly from their folds as if he were preparing to join them. One day, in his second spring, he was missing, and we knew he had joined his own kind. After a few weeks he came back, alighted on the wall, took food from us, and climbed on to my arm. Delighted to see him, we scratched the back of his head and talked to him; but after a few hours he was gone again.

The second time he returned, with a flight of others, he flew down to the wall, but he kept his distance and we had to throw the food to him. He walked away jauntily each time we approached, as if to say, 'So far but no farther; the sky is mine.' He stayed for only a few minutes, and leapt into the air, spreading his wings and flapping away over the tree tops. He had a right to his wildness, and he claimed it, and never came again. But whenever I see jackdaws walking with a swagger over the ploughed land, I pretend that one is Cappy and that if I clap my hands as I used to, one of them will come sailing on the air to me: they all look so alike.

LIZARDS –
JE AND JETTA

WHEN I was small, the word 'lizard' had an unpleasant sound; I imagined something green and slimy. This wrong impression stayed with me until I met a lizard. An aunt by marriage had been rebuilding her grand house, and had added a terrace with a pale stone balustrade. She bought a pair of large, bright-green lizards to off-set the effect, quite believing they would lie around as ornaments. I forget how long (or soon) it was before they disappeared like Herrick's pearls of morning dew. One of them was called Marma-duke (which might have been one good reason for running away), the other 'His Wife', and though ours was a short acquaintance, it changed my thoughts about lizards. They were like jewels.

So when John expressed a wish that he could find a pair, the shock was not so great as it might otherwise have been. All the same, I had a sneaking hope that he never would.

He never did; but some misguided friends of ours were out on a Suffolk heath one spring, and came across a pair of common lizards, sunning themselves on a large stone. It was April, and the creatures were easily caught and brought to us in a perforated tin padded with moss. Had it been a hot summer sun, they would have been far too swift to be taken, for they move with unbelievable speed on a hot day. The female's tail was missing, but the male was a perfect specimen about seven inches long. The ability to shed its tail is the lizard's chief form of protection. On account of its speed it is usually seized by the tail, but what remains with the enemy is not the lizard, but this broken-off tail end, which continues to wriggle and twitch for a short time after the little reptile is free again.

They could not remain in a tin; so by the close of the same day we had put together a vivarium. I say 'put together' advisedly. Here are the materials we used. The base was a piece of the bottom of an old drawer, roughly eighteen inches by twelve. The sides had to be glass so that the lizards could have light and sun, and we could see them. We had had no notice of our visitors' arrival, and sheets of glass do not lie around awaiting unexpected reptiles. There were no shops within reach. After much controversial thought I decided to break up four unpopular pictures. The pieces of glass were not the exact size (few things ever are, I find), but they were near enough for our purpose. A roll of (medicated) adhesive tape from the first-aid box was used to connect the four sides and join them to the base; and to complete it, a sheet of perforated zinc (shaped by bending it) was laid on the top to prevent the lizards' escape. Inside, we covered the floor with two inches of soil, and set in it roots of grass and fern, weeds, pieces of bark, stones and a rock, to make it as like their wild habitat as possible. There was a small hollow cylinder of oak bark which, partly buried, formed a dark tunnel to shelter or sleep in.

We transferred them from their cramped tin, and placed them in their new home on the window-ledge in the sitting-room, where they would get all the available sun. They crawled out of sight and hid themselves for the greater part of several days, rarely coming out to feed.

Twice each day we sprinkled water on to the growing plants, so that Je and Jetta, lately christened, could drink the clinging drops and think them rain (we hoped), and the result was rather like a tropical-plant house. The grass and weeds shot up to spindly heights and had to be trimmed regularly with scissors.

It was doubtful fun collecting their food every day. They never appeared to be gorged, and their shared daily intake was twenty medium-sized spiders, several flies and a number of small grasshoppers. Fortunately we were surrounded by

21

acres of woods in which there were occasional
heaps of old bark and branches, where the supply
of spiders was endless. While they caught and ate
their prey we could examine both lizards. They
were similar in colour, a brownish base overlaid
with pale stripes and spots of varying shades of
green, black, and stone. Je was the prettier, with a
dark stripe between his eyes and a yellowish belly.
After several days we noticed that Jetta had begun
to grow a new tail, but it was smooth, without the
scales such as covered the rest of her body. When
it was fully grown it was still different in texture
and looked as though it might have been stuck on
very neatly.

A lizard's feet are particularly graceful, with
long tapering toes that can spread out and bend
round a stone like a very slim hand. Before attack-
ing an insect it approaches cautiously (swiftly in
the heat, slower when cool) and, when a small
distance away, remains absolutely still, poised and
watching, often with flickering tongue. Immediately before the final lunge, it twitches its tail from
side to side, much as a cat will do when watching
a mouse. Then, with a lightning dart of the head,
the lizard bites its prey, which disappears from
view in several gulps. Wood-spiders are extremely
swift and many times there was quite a chase in
the vivarium.

Sometimes Je and Jetta licked a water-drop
off the glass, and their tongues looked like soft,

minute spade blades. They were always together, and used one another as chin-rests when lying in the sun. They became tame and took insects and water from the tips of our fingers. They played hide-and-seek and chased each other in and out of their miniature jungle.

They sloughed their skins every three or four weeks. The skin cracked first at the sides of the mouth and on the fingers, and then at the back of the neck. They rubbed themselves against the grasses and squeezed themselves under things, so loosening the outer transparent skin from which they eventually wriggled. Sloughing is essential to them, to allow for growth; actually it is that they become too fat and split their outer covering. We had a grass snake once who found it too difficult in captivity to get rid of her skin and we had to let her go wild to free herself.

Their bodies were beautifully bright for a few days each time a skin had been discarded, especially Je's, and after several changes, we discovered that scales had formed on Jetta's new tailpiece, and she was very handsome again as she lay in the sun flattening herself like a little pancake to absorb the heat.

One sunny morning I was watching them when I saw what I thought must be a fight. Je had Jetta by the side of her throat, but she put up no fight, though she tried rather half-heartedly to shake him off. Then he let her go and slid away with an apparent loss of interest. Later in the day I saw Jetta basking in the sun, and Je stealthily approaching from behind a tuft of coarse grass. Suddenly he flicked his tail and lunged at her, grabbing her at the side of the head with his open jaws. He held her there, lashing his tail and making himself out to be no end of a fellow, then dragged her along the ground. Then he let her go again, and himself joined in the basking.

I was rather alarmed about this and told John when he arrived home from school. 'Oh that's all right. It's only a courting display. He doesn't hurt her.'

This was true enough, and, though I did not see the mating, we noticed Jetta becoming stouter and slower and fed her accordingly. She kept more in the shade and appeared less often, living mostly in the bark tunnel.

Then at feeding-time one evening I saw four baby lizards, inch-long and almost black, moving quite swiftly among the grasses. They looked as though they were wearing finely woven coats-of-mail, black in the shadows and bronze in the sun. Their grace was incredible, and the same evening we gave them tiny spiders, which they attacked and ate as though they were old hands at the game.

I scratched on the tunnel and Jetta crawled out, but with great effort. She was exhausted, and refused food or drink, soon turning and dragging herself back to her shelter.

After a few days, however, she was again sleek and swift and had fully recovered. We found one of the babies dead on the second day, but the other three showed amazing energy and precision when hunting, which they appeared to do most of the day. We had a suspicion that Je might eat one of these obviously irritating little creatures, mistaking their identity, or for some best-forgotten reason. He watched them and stalked them exactly as he did the spiders. So four more unworthy pictures fell under our destructive hands, and we built another equally arresting vivarium for the youngsters.

They all flourished throughout the summer, and many children came to see them and loved watching their antics. My dislike of lizards had been only ignorance. I grew to like them very much and was sad in September, when, thinking they might not survive the winter in captivity, we took them on a warm morning to a deep grassy bank with southern exposure, and turned them loose – the young ones twenty feet away from the adults. They were strong and healthy and had always hunted their own kill, so there was every reason to suppose that they would lead their normal wild life again.

We saw Je not far from where we had left him, the following April. He was the only one we saw, and it was only once, but it told us he had survived the winter, and we hoped it was true of Jetta and her fascinating brood. We were not professional zoologists, and had to play many parts by ear, as they say; but one can't go very far wrong by giving animals the type of habitat, food and routine which they would have in their wild freedom.

TAWNY,
AN INJURED OWL

WESTMORLAND is a beautiful but bleak and wet county, and perhaps the birds there are tougher than those in the south-east; which might account for the survival of the owl in this story.

Before we were posted to Suffolk, we lived in a cottage which overlooked the valley of the River Eden, and, though fourteen miles away, we could see plainly the Pennine peak known as Cross Fell. It was a half-mile to the next cottage, so we were surprised one afternoon when we returned from a short walk, to find a cardboard box on our bird table. No note, no address.

We lifted the box down and opened it carefully; it was so light. Inside, there was a tawny owl. It looked dead, it was so still, with closed eyes. John put both hands loosely round it, pinning its wings, and lifted it out. It blinked its lids sleepily but made no movement. It did not take us many seconds to find out what was wrong. Its right wing was practically severed, hanging from a broken shoulder-bone.

A tawny owl is a lovely creature. Its head and body are covered with soft, downy feathers lighter in weight than any other bird's, and so thick that he seems large and fat. His eyes when opened wide are brown, circular and unbelievably beautiful. In certain lights they glow red, like hot coals. The owls' legs and powerful, graceful feet are covered with short, furry feathers, leaving only the claws bare. Their great wing-span helps them to glide through the air, and they make no noise with their wings. They are the friend of man, living on rats and mice, and they should never be shot or destroyed, as they often are by ignorant people who think they are vermin.

Back to my story. In a few days we found out how Tawny had come to be there. John was then nine years old and loved birds above all things, so when a village child found the owl at the side of the road, unable to fly, his wing torn and bleeding, his first thought was to find John. We never knew what had happened, but we thought the bird must have flown into telegraph wires and become entangled.

We took him indoors and examined him. There was nothing one could do but cut off his wing and wash the large wound on his shoulder with warm water and disinfectant. I put on a glove, and he curled his claws round one finger and sat quite still, as if he could feel nothing and had no interest in what was happening. He was too shocked to know.

After we had done what we could, we decided he must have food and drink. But what? He was a bird of prey. John rode as fast as he could to the village on a pony and went from farmer's door to farmer's door asking for mice or rats. These are common enough on farms, but no-one keeps them hanging around once they are caught. He managed to bring back one fresh dead mouse, however, and he chopped it up and pushed it down Tawny's throat. Then I gave him several teaspoonfuls of warm milk and put him back into his box with plenty of hay under him to keep him warm.

The next morning several children arrived with rats and mice (in fact, they always kept up the supply while we needed them). So we chopped up another mouse and pushed it down the throat of the injured bird, who was still alive and seemed slightly stronger than he had been the previous evening. An owl has a huge mouth, which goes far back into the feathers. They swallow mice whole when they are well, usually taking several gulps before the tip of the tail has disappeared. But he was an invalid and we chopped his food for a few days.

He ate and slept by turns and he was getting better, so we knew he could not be kept in a box much longer. By the end of a week we had built him an aviary outside. One side was the house wall, one side was the byre wall, and the two remaining sides were of wire netting supported by posts cut from the small branches of a tree growing in our ghyll. The 'roof' was also of wire. On the floor at the byre end of the aviary we put a large box of hay with a hole in the side, for sheltering and sleeping. We put pieces of rock and stone on the ground on to which he could hop, and sank a large bowl of water into his grass to look like a pond. Then we carried him out and put him into his own estate. He stood, immensely dignified, and blinked his huge eyes slowly, showing the down-covered lids. He obviously liked it, and jumped straight through the hole into the box, knowing instinctively that he was safe there.

As the days went by he became well and strong, and we threw his mouse to him whole. He immediately pounced on it and clutched it with his claws, but we never saw him eat one. He would wait, standing as still as a statue with it, until we had gone away. Sometimes we went indoors to the window overlooking his cage, and peeped at him from behind the curtain, but always, no matter how silent and cautious we were, he would see us first and would watch, his great round eyes full on the window, waiting for us to leave him alone. He lived with us for months but never let us see him eat his prey.

In several weeks he grew friendly and lost all fear of us. He ignored Game, our bull-terrier; she was used to our wild patients and was quite happy to see another, once a really good smell of them had been taken.

Tawny had many visitors. His wound healed, but under his feathers there was always the bare flesh where his wing had joined his body, and of course he could never fly again; but he bathed and preened, and twice we heard him call, as if he were trying out his voice.

After several months we went to Stoneriggs, a farm on the Fells, for a holiday. Tawny had to go with us, and I sat in the front seat of the car all the way, with Tawny on my hand and Game between my knees. The driver was beside me, and in the back of the car were my two boys, John and Ivan, and lots of luggage. Tawny's eyes were only open to the size of large slits, and the rims were redder than usual, so we knew he was not altogether pleased with the experience. But he showed no other sign, and did not attempt to hop down or flutter his wing. It is the intense stillness of an owl that is so disarming.

We arrived safely, and Tawny was housed in a loft, where he could catch his own rats and mice. There were sacks of grain for him to perch on, a dry, wood floor, and that warm atmosphere a farm loft has. He loved it, and came to us in friendly leaps when we visited him daily. At the end of two

uneventful weeks we took him home with us in the same way we had taken him there, and he seemed content to be put back into his own aviary. But a few days later, when I was outside watching him, I saw that he was ill – dull, half-closed eyes and laboured breathing, although he had appeared to be normal at his morning feed.

I took him on to my hand and carried him into the house. When I examined him, I found a new, inflamed scar on his injured shoulder. It was 'angry' and hot, and it was soon obvious that Tawny was dying. He must have been bitten by one of the rats he killed at Stoneriggs, and it had turned septic. It is difficult to see that a bird is ill if he eats normally – his feathers cover so much. He must have been ill for days without our knowing.

He died the next morning in the cardboard box of hay, but he had been much loved, and had seemed to like his strange life.

That adventure had a sad ending, but last year in Suffolk we found two deserted owlets in the bole of a hollow elm tree. Their mother had probably been shot or trapped by the gamekeeper, Josh. He was a lovable but ignorant old man, whose sole reply was: 'You can't tell me them things do na good,' when spoken to about *any* of the victims that he hung on his gibbet under the beech trees.

We had watched this owl from the time she laid her round white eggs until the day she did not return. The next morning, the two orphans, hungry with waiting, were opening their gigantic mouths to each other and nibbling beaks, asking to be fed. We soon had a ladder there and brought them home. And then the question was: where were they to live?

Our woodshed was thatched, with three wooden sides, and a fourth of wire netting with a door. John and I looked at each other and had the same idea. The shed was soon stripped of its woodpile and some coal, and we fastened rough branches at varying heights, put a large box, with a hole in its side, high in the top corner of the aviary, and turned them into it. It might have been made for them, literally!

They lived on bits of raw rabbit (given with fur and bone), mice and chopped rat. In a very short time they were flying to the wire as soon as they saw us approaching, and they fastened on the food we held, immediately we were inside the door of the aviary. This became painful, and we had second thoughts about it and wore gloves.

We did not attempt to make pets of them, because as soon as they were fully grown and could catch food we intended to release them into the woods, their natural home. This did not take many weeks, and one lovely morning we carried them out and let them go together. For several days we put food on the roof of their cage, in case they came back to feed, but it was not taken, so we knew they were finding their own. They had been fun to handle and observe, and had distinct characteristics though they were so young. The male was smaller and more tame; the female was very wary: she would walk quietly into her box, turn and stand in the doorway, regarding us with a cold stare, and then walk out again; and back, and out, and so on every time she was fed. The male stayed, hopped around or flew, not minding whether we stayed or went, so long as his crop was full; but had we produced another mouse suddenly, it would have been swooped on and snatched away in a split second. One has to be wide awake when dealing with wild birds, and ready for any emergency.

Talking of being wide awake, as soon as it is dusk, three wild owlets come and sit in the tree outside my bedroom window every night. They like the short grass of the lawn now that it is high summer and the wild grasses and flowers are so tall. They may be the young ones who were being taught to hunt at night from the same window ledge weeks ago. It was bright moonlight; multiple whispered *seep*s – soft, unidentifiable – woke me, and I got out of bed to trace them. There was one adult owl with several young flying backwards and forwards from the sill to the stable roof; they appeared to go two at a time, the parent bird taking one youngster. The soft hissing noises continued all the time, and there was an extra

flurry each time the owl returned to change pupils. I watched, hidden behind the curtains, for some time, but I tired first and left them to their exercises. I fell asleep listening to the whispers that had wakened me.

I have been asked many times if an owl is *really* wise, but I have never given an opinion in case I meet another one. He is dignified, sedate and cautious, and knows how to sit very still; he waits and watches and misses nothing that he wants to see; and if he were dressed in cap and gown and walked up the Oxford High, I have a feeling that his wisdom would be taken for granted.

SQUIRRELS

Neat as a nut
Soft as a scut,
Pert as a robin
Taut as a strut;

Lithe as a cat
Sure as a bat,
All tail and ear-tufts,
Enchanting, he sat.

I SUPPOSE that most people's thoughts about a squirrel are of a picture-book variety: a ball of fur, sweet and a little playful, and quite willing to be anything to anybody. The squirrels that I have known were nothing like that. They were wilful and determined, and did exactly as they liked. They grumbled in no uncertain language; all except one, and he had been lost and very ill and we had nursed him back to health; my hands were his friends and he showed them affection and obedience. But that was the only one (more about him later).

There was a little fellow with only half a tail who lived near our hen-run. He found it difficult to swing and climb. He was fairly tame, and came to within a few yards of our chairs in summer. We nailed a small board to an oak tree, and supplemented his rations by putting chopped apple and bread soaked in milk there for him. One day I heard squeals and ran out in time to frighten away a stoat, and see the little stump-tail race up the tree. The stoat might have followed him had I not been there. Only a few days ago I watched a stoat come down a tree head first, which is unusual: they usually come down backwards. They go up in search of young birds and baby squirrels, but not often, I think.

The first squirrel we had was a bundle of wrath. A gamekeeper had caught her in a wire rabbit-snare, and he brought her to the door in a sack, the wire still round her swollen neck. We freed her from it, nursed and fed her for a fortnight, keeping her in an especially wired outdoor shed, but she did little except race up and down the wire and swear at us, though she had boughs and leaves to play on and a nesting-box for retiring. She had not a good word for any of us (perhaps to her we were part of the snare). When she was strong again we carried her into the beech copse and watched her bound away. Catching her had been like trying to catch lightning, and she had to be boxed before we could hold her.

I am writing this in March: the late snow has gone, the woods are sodden, the trees bare of all foliage, their feathered tops brushing the sky. I can see large nests, shaped like footballs, lodged in supporting twigs. These are squirrel dreys. They are all similar, but the materials they are made from differ. They may have a few birch twigs at the base, and be woven of dead grasses, honeysuckle 'rope' and beech leaves; they are lined with warmer gleanings, rabbit fluff, honeysuckle bark chewed very thin, and feathers. The squirrel enters through a loosely woven patch in one wall. Not content with one winter residence, he has up to four other roughish ones in the same area. He does not hibernate, but retires into his drey in wet or windy weather and sleeps, emerging on mild days for food and exercise. Once, we found one's tracks in the snow: he had come down the tree, run about five yards, and then, after sitting to ponder long enough to make a small depression in the snow, had changed his mind and run back up the tree.

Squirrels are often seen in pairs in winter, but I think they sleep in separate dreys. Their sleep is lighter than that of the hibernating dormouse and hedgehog, and they soon wake if disturbed. They grow special winter coats of long brown-grey hair, with ear-tufts and bushy tails.

Before I say any more, I must tell you that we are lucky enough to live in a district of red squirrels, where the pirate greys have not yet appeared. So in peace they bury their nuts and acorns during autumn, and though they do not remember where they put them, they scratch about and scent them later in winter.

In Suffolk the first babies are born about April Fool's Day. Usually there are up to four, naked and blind, and the drey lining is extra soft and warm to receive them. Occasionally there is a second litter about July or August, and our waif, Rusty, must have come from one of these. When I found him, lost and hungry, sitting on a fallen birch branch, I thought there must be something seriously amiss with him, and when he allowed me to pick him up without resisting, it looked hopeless.

Sometimes a squirrel will be leaping over the leaves, scratching them at intervals, bounding up a tree trunk, swinging into a hazel bush and down to the ground again, unaware that one of us is approaching. Suddenly he will realise that he is not alone, and with one swift scurry will be high above the reach of man, from where he can peer down and growl his disapproval before ascending still further to his own tree-top kingdom. Squirrels are intensely alert, swift creatures with jerky movements that confuse a human being unused to their tricks. In the house, a chair will be stormed in amazing speed of action: a little face peeps over the back, then vanishes, to reappear from under the seat in the time one takes to draw a breath.

The sight of a sleepy, indifferent baby squirrel so near the ground on a clear day in October, was therefore cause for concern. We found it had no broken bones. It allowed itself to be carried into the house and set down on a rug, before it took fright and hurried into a corner, where it sat watching us with dull eyes, quite unlike the bright beads of a healthy squirrel.

Within a few minutes he had fallen forwards on to the tip of his nose, and looked like a toy that had been thrown down by a child. I mixed a small amount of warmed milk and brown bread in an egg-cup, added a spot of brandy, picked him up and cupped him in my lap on an apron. Gently opening his mouth with a matchstick, I fed him from a salt-spoon. This took some time, and showers of milk were sneezed out over us both before we decided he had had enough for his first meal.

Although he was overwhelmingly tired, he was frightened too, and between mouthfuls he tried to hide his face by curling his head into the fur between his forelegs.

For a nest he had an old sheepskin glove lined with wool, and this was his chosen bed all the time that he was with us. At first, for safety, we put it into a box, which we kept covered and warm, and never did he try to get out alone, or even uncover himself. Tightly wound into a ball, he slept for the whole of the time between meals, and for twelve hours at a stretch during the nights. This saved his life, I think: eating and sleeping, eating and sleeping, dryness and warmth, gave their reward. His bones were less sharp to the touch, he filled out his jacket better; his eyes grew brighter, and he loved his salt-spoon and egg-cup. At the sight of them, he tried to climb out of my hands and snatch at them. He used his forefeet to hold his spoon and fed from it quite steadily. My lap and apron were his sanctuary, and on them he was fearless.

One day he had eaten his breakfast and washed his face, when he suddenly ran up the outside of my sleeve and sat on my shoulder, where he finished his toilet. When I put up my hand to take him down, the fun began. Clinging to my clothes, he ran down my back, across my skirt and up again on to the other shoulder. This went on for minutes, until he was tired and let me catch him. He was soon back in his glove, and I knew that he would need watching more in the future.

But his nose constantly needed wiping: he was not yet healthy. One day he had an ache too, and crawled around on his belly to ease himself. It looked at one time as though he would die, in spite of his improved outlook on life and his attempts to be normal. His illness, whatever it was, was beating us.

43

So during the next few days I kept him wrapped in a square of flannel, and carried him inside my shirt-blouse next to my skin, so that he would get constant warmth. We fed him on raw yolk of egg with an added suspicion of brandy, and very little else, until his pain stopped. And it did stop, quite suddenly; and he became a darting, mischievous puff of speed.

He sampled all the furniture, flowers, leaves, rugs. He looked into all the rooms, tried to scale the walls (and looked very surprised when he slid down, unable to get a foothold), and hid under chests. He crawled under the bedclothes and searched for nuts. He perched on the tops of our heads or explored our pockets, and the only real peace we had was when he was asleep.

Game was his friend. She had licked him clean when he was too ill to care and the egg had stuck to his whiskers. He had grown used to the dog's kind tongue-wash. We sometimes thought that Game considered this undisciplined child was being allowed too many liberties, and of course he was! But his pranks and good spirits were entrancing to watch, and we were so glad that he had lived.

It was by this time late autumn, and there was no question of turning him into the woods again. We had come to the conclusion that he had either fallen or strayed from the drey and been forsaken. He was too young to have been able to feed himself before we found him. So he would have to be kept as a pet for the rest of his life, a state which, to judge from his reactions, would cause him no alarm. But, owing to circumstances, it was impossible for me to keep him for very long, and John was going away hawking for some time.

When Rusty was quite better I telephoned a friend of ours who wanted a squirrel. He was a middle-aged farmer, used to handling animals of all kinds. Any creature would be understood by him.

'Do you still want a squirrel?' Well, he wasn't sure . . . Where was it? . . . What was it? . . . How was it? . . . Was it house-trained? . . . Had it any vices? He came to see for himself, and half an hour of watching this red ball of energy convinced our friend that here indeed was a gem.

As they drove away, with Rusty in his old glove, we had mixed feelings about it all. He was such an alive little creature, and he left a very empty box behind him. He had never bitten us, nor even grumbled, and because of his slender immaturity he was exquisite to watch.

Some weeks later his owner was very ill, and confined to bed for several months. I went over to see him one spring afternoon, and sat by his bed chatting to him. 'And how is Rusty?' I asked him. He put his hand under the bedclothes and from the side of his knees drew out the little animal, curled up, asleep. 'Fine.' Rusty opened his eyes, yawned, and sat up on his master's hand. I took him into mine and stroked him. Anyone else could have done the same. He was relaxed and contented, and it was his sleep time; when I set him down, he ran back to his dark, warm nest by the invalid's knees.

Most of the time he lived in a large cage in the bedroom, containing a sleeping box and earth – the door was left open so that he was not imprisoned. Sometimes he took a turn in the outdoor aviary, but not from choice; he loved human companionship. His clean habits were natural and he had needed no training; he even had no fleas, and wild squirrels are usually plagued with them.

Of course, Rusty's was an unusual case. We see numbers of squirrels all through the year. There is a pair to every ten acres here, and one morning, through the window, I saw five; three were playing, chasing each other up and down a beech tree, and two odd ones were a few yards away, leaping over the leaves.

If you remain still and noiseless you can watch them in their own surroundings – much more fun than seeing them through bars at a zoo. But you have to be patient and quiet. Children often come into the woods in spring and summer, carrying sticks to hit the trees and bracken as they pass. I wonder how many of them have seen a squirrel, though doubtless somewhere above them has been one, stamping his feet on the bark, lashing his tail in wild curves, and swearing – '*Ski-wow-wow*' in anger and alarm at the noise and commotion below.

VIXEN

A DITCH surrounds the garden, and it rarely contains much water. The banks are bedded with primroses and violets in the spring, and the rest of the year grass grows and is cut in keeping with the almost circular lawn. Then the rabbit-holes become very obvious; man's inhumanity in the form of myxomatosis had not reached here then. Game liked one of these holes in particular: it was sandy, and it was easy to scratch away the entrance and send showers of it flying behind her. It was about fifteen yards from the sitting-room window, and one could see into it from the bedroom window above.

One day in late February I noticed that the earth at the entrance was flattened, and there were other paw-marks than Game's. She, when I examined it, behaved strangely, stiffening slightly, and strutting by suspiciously without entering. 'John.' And when he came, 'What do you make of this?' He knelt down, and put his head as far into the hole as he could. 'Fox. Stinks of it. Let's leave it alone and watch for a day or two.'

We did, and it was obvious that it was being used as a hide-out regularly, but never a sight of a fox coming or going. A week passed, and he examined it again. 'Still there, and it is stronger.' So one late afternoon I went upstairs and took up my position at the window; dusk might prove something. I waited for exactly two hours, watching, until no shape was really distinguishable any longer: no movement of any kind.

The next evening I did the same again. After about ninety minutes, there she stood on top of the bank. She had stolen out so stealthily and leapt up with such ease and speed, that though my eyes had been trained on the hole I had not seen her leave. She paused for a moment, glanced around, and walked, with the light, indescribable grace foxes have, quickly up the ride leading from the ditch at that point. After a few yards she turned and looked behind her, stood still, watched, walked on. And so up the ride and out of sight. I was delighted; she would come back; but not while I waited that day.

One afternoon I saw her slip into her earth as easily as she had left it, with as little exertion as one uses to draw a line on a page. (It takes gymnasts years of training to acquire the precision of movement a fox is born with; they never can acquire its grace and agility.)

Imagination is soon fired, and we pictured the cubs as they would be; we were even planning their protection; if only the Hunt did not find her, this elusive, lovely vixen.

Rabbits still ran around the lawn, and pheasants strutted by a felled oak within three yards of her entrance. Foxes are wise enough not to kill on their own doorstep and so arouse suspicion. I had heard this, and now believed it. Our hens, who ran wild, were untouched.

The woodsmen passed over her every morning and evening. They lit a fire near the oak and sat there to have their breakfasts. But they had no idea of our knowledge. They were on the wrong side of the ditch for that. She must have heard them talking, as she heard our voices and sounds from the house. I sometimes crept near enough to see whether the earth held her marks still. It did, and one could smell fox. By this time John had gone away on a hawking trip again, and I was left to notice developments.

It was March. A dry frost during the night had deepened the blue of the morning sky and sharpened the sun. Last year's growth of dead grass was still in the clearing surrounding the ditch. So I got out the grass-hook and long rake and prepared to tackle the rather soggy land. It was elevenish. A woodpecker tapped loudly on a hollow tree, and the clap of pigeons' wings disturbed the peace, but there was no other sound. Three days before, the Hunt had been through the woods but had drawn a blank. I had heard them but had not seen them.

Our vixen must have been curled securely in her earth. As I worked I imagined her still there. What a lovely day; what a lovely world.

Suddenly in the far distance a hound gave tongue; then others; and others. Another Hunt was on, far away, far enough away – perhaps they were heading for the Big Wood, or upper Waxhall, but not here again so soon.

I slashed and raked, every yard or so turning to admire the altered look, and as I gathered one heap of dead leaves, I touched a round ball of fur, about as big as a tangerine. I picked it up and examined it. One shut eye-slit was visible, and one side of a closed pink mouth. Its breathing was even and undisturbed. It was a dormouse. I put it into my pocket and finished that patch of ground, then replaced the still-sleeping mouse and covered him with leaves.

The baying of hounds again. Nearer. Perhaps by this time only a quarter of a mile away, and every moment nearer still. I put down my tools and called Game into the house, shutting the doors. I called the hens into their enclosure.

By now there was no doubt. They were giving chase. The baying and excited whimpering and yapping was travelling fast through the trees, but seemed to be following the outer edge of the woods, away from us.

I was fastening the wire gate of the hen-run on the clearing's edge when it happened: as if straight out of the ground at my feet, a dozen hounds appeared, sniffing, lolloping, running, leaping, while the rest were only a few yards away, baying and streaking along through the trees.

I ran into the open. Suddenly I knew. They were in full cry, though I could see no prey. In and out of the trees, through bracken and bramble, heads low, tails waving like flag-poles, hot on the scent of what? They had almost reached the cart-track that flanks the woods, when the vixen broke clear of the trees, leapt a ditch, crossed the track and cut through a low hedge into the ploughed field, with the hounds only twenty feet behind her. She looked so slight, and her brush looked too heavy as she raced, at full stretch, across the furrows of the heavy, wet earth. 'Run, run!' I called, and I found that I was biting the knuckles of my hand.

The first few hounds were following her. There surely could be no hope. But their muzzles were to the ground, and hers was straight out. She was running, guided by her eyes, over ground she knew. They were following her only by scent. And the ploughed land did not help them there. The distance between hunted and hunter was lengthening.

The pounding thud of scores of hooves galloping into the clearing and into the lane; the shouts of excited followers, and the blowing of that undeniable horn. Most of the following-on hounds were hopelessly at sea, all scents now being mixed and trodden into the earth, those first few yards of ploughed earth. Those nearest the vixen had lost her. She had streaked into the next half-field of uncut kale and was hiding there, getting her breath, watching, perhaps needling her way up the length of the lanes of thick stalks that had given her shelter and a chance to live.

Things happen so quickly in a hunt. In a split second a scene can change, excitement be born or die. So it was now.

'Did you see her? Did you see where she went?'

'No,' I shouted.

She was still in that kale, and only a narrow field away. Give her time, give her time.

Many of the hounds, confused, set off down the lane towards the road. The huntsman cantered after them, sounding his horn. The rest of the field, who had reined in their horses, now urged them to follow, talking, laughing, on the verge of a thrill they had missed, thanks to the thick woods the vixen had chosen for her cover in escape.

As they turned from me to the west, I too turned, to the north-east, and with my eyes searched the upper far fields which began where the kale ended. As I watched, a belated elderly follower galloped towards me from the beech copse.

'What happened? Where did they go?'

'Nothing happened. Down the lane and across the road into Tinker's.'

'Right, thanks.' And another had drawn his own wrong conclusions.

Now, all the hounds had drawn away from the kale, and were off after the horses. I saw a neighbour standing in his cottage garden, at the lower end of the kale field. Perhaps he had seen what I had missed? I half walked, half ran down the cart-track until we were within shouting distance.

'Did you see her?'

'Yis, yis,' he called 'and she was out o' top kale heading for Breach while they was up yonder wi' you.'

We laughed, and I turned and walked back, happy and sad. Some may think it fun to hunt a fox, but every man to his taste, and my fun is to see an escape. The sly skill of a small wild animal outwitting hounds and men, and giving them the slip when hope seemed foolish, was a thrill I shall never forget.

'Good lass,' my heart called to her as I walked back to my ditch. 'Good lass!'

It was over. They were not likely to pass the same way twice in a day. Occasionally I raised my head, and in the distance, beyond the ploughed land, I saw the pink coats and heard scarcely visible hounds give tongue.

I have no proof that it was our vixen; but the earth that had housed her was deserted from that day.

Once, in the night, I heard what I hoped was she, lapping water from the stone bowl on the lawn under my window. But she chose another place for her safety. The rabbits have reclaimed their home, and Game showers the sand over us again, as she digs for them.

I have heard it said, in defence, that a fox enjoys being hunted. When a vixen can speak, I shall be ready to accept her comment. Until then, I shall think my thoughts and believe what I have witnessed.

WEASELS

WE WERE often called upon suddenly to provide living-accommodation made from the odd collection of scraps we possessed. When you live miles from a town, there is no question of being able to 'run to the shop'. By rallitrap, drawn by our Welsh mare, Molly, town was an hour's journey, and then ten minutes for stabling at the George.

When these contingencies threatened, we had to look at one another and say, 'What have we that would *do*?' We certainly could never keep any tools of any worth. Boys (most) have a knack of being able to lose, rust or break a tool in just under the record time. So I insisted that the essential pieces were not allowed out of doors: they were a bushman's saw, a screwdriver, a mallet and a pair of pliers. We never did keep a hammer. The last we possessed 'happened to fall into the well'. So with this meagre set we had to furnish any type of animal dwelling at any unknown minute.

We had a disused goat-shed, where we dumped old wood, glass, pieces of wire, cardboard, cages, traps, rope, nails, old fencing, and other oddments from which we should sooner or later be fashioning. An emergency call found us standing in this shed, pondering, and searching, and thinking none too slowly. Each time it happened it looked as if we really had used up all our available resources. Yet we never had.

I remember that I was having tea alone. John was later than I expected, and there was no point in waiting for him. I had finished, and was about to move from the table, when I saw him pass the window, beaming broadly. He did not wait to remove his coat, but walked into the dining-room carrying a small cube-shaped tin tied with string. He put it on the table in front of me: 'Guess what! But don't touch.' From his obvious pleasure I might have guessed, 'The Hope diamond.' I might. He supplied his own answer: 'Baby weasels.' They had been brought to his friend Guy Aylmer by a farm worker who had found a nest of four weasel kits in the base of a stack at threshing time.

The only weasel I had seen near-to was in the long meadow here, and Game had nosed it out. It was the fastest-moving little creature I had seen. First it jumped into the air in front of her and spun on its hind legs. Then it leapt along for several feet (perhaps yards) with a startled Game in pursuit. As she was nearly within biting distance the weasel jumped again, sprang, and twirled and threw itself into the air while Game stopped, ears pricked, eyes keen, fascinated and bewildered. Then another few yards, and so on, until it gained the ditch and disappeared.

This flashed through my mind as I beheld the tin. 'They're wonderful little things. You'll love them. The Major found them in a nest. His ferret has been suckling them, but they are too many for her with her own litter, and I am going to rear these two by hand. They do smell rather awful, so don't take the lid off.'

The last injunction was quite unnecessary. I reasoned, cajoled, then protested rather limply, because it was hopeless from the start. There is only one reply to 'We can't let them die.' So after a complicated tea interval we found ourselves in the goat-shed, the interior of which always looked as if a bomb had just exploded in it. Actually, this confusion helped – one could see practically everything at once!

By bedtime, a secure box, thirty-six inches by twelve, with a small-meshed wire front, had been made to house them. It would serve until morning, and we put their tin inside for them to sleep in. John took one out to show me. It bit his hand with its minute teeth, and spat at us with a noise like a sneeze. But its heart-shaped face with those bright bead-eyes, broad ears and sensitive

wet nozzle was disarming. The body (nut-brown with cream underparts) was about three inches long, with an inch-and-a-half brown tail. Although so small, the kit showed intense energy and viciousness, and exuded the most revolting smell in self-protection. When John replaced it it spat again and darted into its tin. That was the male. The female was slightly lighter in colour and even more vicious. He became less alien towards us in a very short time; she was never even civil.

The next day, John completed the house: it had a sliding door, near to the top of one side. A sleeping-compartment was fixed to the inside of the roof, and had a half-crown-sized hole for the entrance, with a step-ladder leading up to it; there was a shelf they could jump to, and a hollow log and pipe they could run through or hide in; they had a branch to swing from and a sliding tray for their floor (cleanliness is essential). Their house was placed on the flat doors covering our well, and under cover of the well-roof, so that we could watch them unseen from the dining-room and kitchen windows.

We soon began to call them the Wizzles, on account of their antics. Except when they were eating or sleeping, they spent their entire time in play. This consisted of leaping about; pouncing on each other; hiding in the pipe and then dashing out and jumping as far up the box-side as possible and falling down again; turning somersaults; leaping at the wire; pulling each other out of the sleeping-room and off the ladder. It was all done with the greatest alacrity, and we laughed more at them than at any animals before or since. One day, the Wizzle inside the sleeping-room was leaning out, holding the other by the back of his neck, dangling from the hole. The contortions of the victim were unbelievably adroit; though swinging like a hurried pendulum, he screwed himself into every letter of the alphabet before he was finally dropped, to race up the ladder and continue the game unseen in the box.

They wound themselves in balls, like kittens, to sleep, but at the slightest disturbance twitched and spat before they were fully awake. John fed them always. He had purposely placed their door near the top of the side of their box to avoid an escape when the door was opened. They lived on mice, sparrows, pieces of rabbit, bread and milk, and water. They preferred not to eat in the open if

61

anyone were around, and dragged their food into their upstairs compartment. It was most funny when the joint they were carrying was too big to go through the hole. They became angry with it, and pulled and spat and dropped it, then darted down the steps, or took a flying jump to retrieve it and try again.

The male soon allowed himself to be picked up without too much dashing about first. They both ceased to bite. John's was the only hand that touched them, and, since it was the source of all their supplies, they came to respect it.

They grew during the summer and remained in boisterous health. They had been in an ideal position, always outdoors, but shaded and dry, with roomy quarters, and with each other for exercise and companionship. Their essential characteristics had been unaltered by captivity. They ceased to mind when we watched them, and we sometimes sat on the well-top, while they wrestled and hid and struggled and ignored their audience.

About the middle of September we knew they must be allowed to go free. They were fully grown wild creatures. So one fine morning, John put them into their original tin (a tricky operation) and carried them through the woods into a far meadow, where there was a ditch and plenty of hedge-covering. He opened the lid after putting the tin on the ground. When they had recovered from the surprise they did not scamper away, as one would have expected, but ran quite cautiously to the banks of the ditch, and disappeared.

The well-top looked deserted for a long time after their return to the wild; we had got used to the darting movements of the healthy little creatures and it took time to forget them. We scrubbed their house and stored it in the goat-shed to be ready for the next emergency; there was bound to be one, because there always was, with regularity.

HOBBY
(FEATHERED)

THEY HAD been turning out the stuffed birds in the bothy in the grounds of Culford School. There was quite a collection of stuffed birds and John had been asked to label them. One of them looked as though it had been sparring with a piece of barbed wire, and was given to him to bring home. It was a hobby (a member of the hawk family about the size of a kestrel).

It was a few weeks later, at the beginning of the summer: we had some newly hatched ducklings, and I had put them with an old broody hen in a chicken-run on the lawn. I was watching them, when I saw Penelope Purdown, our Siamese cat, walk stealthily towards the duckling house. She leapt up on to it and lay watching the yellow mites running back and forth. She looked enchanted, and shot out a hind leg and licked it in that inconsequential way cats have. She stopped, and watched again. She gradually changed her position to that of any member of the cat tribe before it springs – feet and body pressed to the earth, tail slowly moving from side to side, with an occasional conscious twitch.

I was thinking it was about time I fetched her away, having already called her and been ignored, when Game's mother, our brindled bull-terrier bitch named Cherry Brandy, jumped up from lying beside me, ran down the lawn, took Penelope by the back of the neck, and dragged her to my feet. I was astonished, first by the dog's action, and second because Penny let her do it without resistance. Penelope calmly walked back and took up her position again. The bitch stood and watched her, looking almost as surprised as I felt. When Penelope's tail started to lash, off went the bitch and collared her and dragged her back to me again.

I fondled and praised the bitch, and carried the erring Siamese into the house. I was wishing very much that one of the children could have been with me to see this happen, when John appeared. 'Tom says there is a hawk that keeps coming into the stack-yard and he is going to shoot it. He says, "When I see him again it'll be the last time." I wonder if it *will* come again.' Tom was the farm foreman, and a great friend to us all. He kept a gun in the barn and in his own words he only ever needed one cartridge. (When we first came to Suffolk he was a little sceptical about any small

boy in and out of his buildings, but as time went on he lost his suspicions, and helped us in our difficulties with strange animals, whom he usually greeted with: 'Oh dear oh dear, another!').

No more was said that day, but the possibilities had been turned over in John's mind by the next day when he walked into the barn: 'Got the hawk yet, Tom?'

'No, but I shall, never fear. Tom'll pin him all right. Yes, yes.' Tom was shutting the great doors, preparing to go out.

'Where are you going, Tom?'

'Hill Farm, but I shan't be there long.' And off he set.

Suddenly, tearing like a wind through the house and upstairs came John. When he came down he had the hobby in his hand, and was grinning like fun. It had a long stick running through the length of its body and protruding six inches beyond the tail; its head could be screwed off. 'I'm going to stick this in the top of the tractor chimney outside the barn for when Tom comes back. He'll shoot it, and I won't half pull his leg.' The tractor stood at the side of one of the stacks, hidden from the view of people swinging round the corner of the road leading into the stackyard. He climbed up, stuck the stick down the pipe, turned the bird's head slightly to make it look more alive, and crept away. 'I shall be in the woodshed. Call me if you see Tom come back? He's bound to be some time yet. What larks!'

I was in the kitchen: 'I'll keep an eye on the yard.' Within a minute of John's leaving me, I walked into the sitting-room for something. I had got halfway across the floor when a shot split the silence. I ran to the back again and outside, and saw what looked like a Red Indian doing a war-dance. Old Josh, the gamekeeper, complete with sacking apron and knee-flaps, was jumping up and down waving the hobby's headless body, shaking his fist at the barn, and hollering, 'It's got a stick in it! I'll have un for this! I'll get un. It's a stuffed un. I'll get un!' and on and on, jigging about in his rage. He was an irascible, boastful old villain, and the farm-workers loved to plague him, which did not improve his peppery temper.

It was one of the funniest sights I ever saw. The prank had completely miscarried, but was far

more effective with Josh than it would have been
with the calm Tom. I ran back, grabbed a shilling,
and went as fast as I could to the old man. I was
laughing as I went – he was still shouting threats
to an absent Tom and a bare stackyard, and John
was keeping well out of the way. 'Josh! Josh be
quiet. It was not intended for you.'

'I'll get un, you'll see. It's a stuffed un, a stuffed
bud.'

'Yes, all right. But be quiet a moment and listen. John put it there for Tom to find when he comes back from Hill Farm. How could he know *you'd* come round the corner at that moment?'

Josh threw the piece of shattered bird on to the ground and wiped the back of his hand across his mouth.

'Here's a drink for you. Now go away and forget all about it.'

I thrust the shilling into his hand, and away he went, muttering and fidgeting in his unappeased wrath.

I collected the pieces of the hobby, which had been blown in two by the point-blank hit, and was climbing up to replace it, when out of the corner of my eye I caught a movement at the open wooden shutter of the barn window. I turned and looked: there shone Tom's face, with a grin from ear to ear, red as a hunter's moon, having seen the entire business and laughed himself silly. When I had collected myself, he told me what had happened.

He had gone back into the barn for something, shutting the large doors. While he was in there, John had put the hobby in place, and come away without Tom seeing or hearing him. When Tom emerged, intending to go to Hill Farm, he spotted the 'hawk', ran back into the barn for his gun, and was taking aim when he realized it was not alive. 'I said to myself, "Ho ho, Master John, you don't

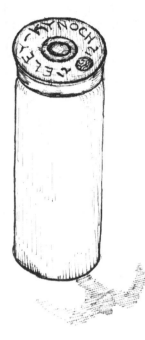

catch Tom with tricks like that, no no."' He went
to replace his gun, and while unloading it he
heard a shot. Josh had come round the corner of
a stack, seen the hobby, and shot it, scarcely
taking aim. He ran and picked it up (watched by
Tom hidden in the barn), only to discover it was
stuffed. His anger and dance and my explanation
were all heard by Tom, who got far more fun out
of it than any of us.

We were still chuckling when we went to bed.
Josh had a drink in the local inn, where the story

went the rounds for many nights (Tom saw to that). Josh retired a year ago, but the question he disliked most, from any of his workmates, was: 'Shot any more hawks, Josh?'

Somehow the original culprit sparrow-hawk was forgotten. I never heard that Tom's one cartridge had been used on him. Maybe he had also been an onlooker, and had split his sides doing whatever a hawk does when he wants to laugh?

MALLARD AND CO.

'Ever had any mallards, John?'
'No.'
'Would you like some?'
'Oh, yes please.'
'Right. Come on and let's find you a pair.'

J UST THAT. And I had listened myself into
another episode.
We had been having tea with a farmer friend in
Norfolk, and it was not strange that the conversation had taken the turn it had. These mallards had
flown from the Broads, and alighted among the
Khaki Campbells and Indian Runners that inhabited the Burke stackyard. In the hard weather they
had shared the grain thrown to the tame ducks,
and gradually had become fearless and settled
down. They were treated as ornaments. They laid
eggs and reared young in the spring, but they are
not primarily egg-layers like their domesticated
relations.

It did not take long to secure a drake and two ducks. It was dusk, and they were shuffling down for the night. Our host cradled them in a cardboard box and put it in the car. When we eventually said goodbye and drew out on to the home road, one brain at least was at work devising a temporary shelter for the unexpected arrivals.

A mallard is swift on the wing and flies for the joy of it. I was imagining, perhaps hopefully, that if we did not clip their wings, they would leave us faster than they had arrived. We had one duck house, and an enclosure containing a pond that drained that part of the woods; our small fleet of ducks were Khaki Campbells, with a most truculent drake in charge. Putting the mallards with them was out of the question.

But John had his plans. We left them in their box for the night, and early the next morning he let out the browns, and shut the wilds in the only duck house. One side was of wire netting, so that they could see the landscape and their civilised neighbours, and become used to them in time. We fed and watered them and left their wings intact. We had to drive the tame batch into a stable at night, until we could solve the housing problem.

By great luck, two days after the mallards arrived an old friend from an adjoining village came to see us. We called him Nutkin, seeing that his name was Squirrel. He was an old man, whose heart refused to acknowledge anything but the eternal youth of the present. He had much time for the young who love nature and understood them. Though a retired farmer, he spent his time in voluntarily serving his neighbours. He was a rare and gentle man, saddened by the tragic death of his own grandson.

Nutkin wandered around with John, seeing the stock; and was amused by the mallards. His favourite comment was 'What a coincidence!' It seemed that everything was related to everything else, in his philosophy. So that, when he paused, watched the duck-run, and repeated, 'Mmm . . . what a coincidence,' we knew that a plan was taking shape. 'Don't do anything. I've a tumbril without wheels. It should make a good un if I can alter it the way I think. See: I'll bring it up at the end of the week. Can you manage till then?'

We could, and did, and true to his word he arrived. I saw him coming round the bend of the road leading into our stackyard. He was standing in a tumbril drawn by an old Suffolk Punch that had the roughest harness, with ropes from the halter serving as reins. There was no room for the dear old man to sit, for the 'duck house' fitted spoon-fashion into the tumbril. His brown eyes glowed with pleasure, and his white hair fringed his cap behind. The strange-looking load rumbled slowly nearer, and I thought, 'How on earth can it be got through the garden and the poultry-run gate?' It couldn't. That was certain.

'It's too heavy for us to lift. I think I'd better drive it round the back, and we can drop it over the ditch, or in it, or something. That all right?' with a chuckle. John shot up out of nowhere and joined him and they went round by the field pond, through the meadow, and drew up alongside the hedged ditch separating them from the garden. Obviously this was not my job, and I went indoors thinking, 'Help!' When I went outside again to call them for lunch, a four-foot gap had been cut in the hedge, and the ditch banks were churned, but the duck house was in place. Tom had been called in with spade and crowbar and his fund of common sense.

The shafts and wheels had been removed from the tumbril, and it had been given a slightly convex corrugated-iron roof. Between that and the sides was wire a foot deep, allowing light and air and vision. It had its own wooden floor, and the back (which normally was removable) had been turned into a door. How Nutkin had got it into his current tumbril we never knew. But his coincidence worked, and saved further head-scratching.

Next day John painted the whole a bright green, put a good layer of straw on the floor, and transferred the mallards to it. The hedge was patched up, the banks repaired, and the quiet was patterned again with the noises that only ducks make.

On a bright morning it is a joy to see any duck stretched to its full height spreading its wings and wafting them, lifting itself almost off the ground, then shuffling its tail, relaxing and waddling on. But it is finer to see a drake mallard doing this. He is neatly made and can fly into the sky at will, be he serf or master. The sheen on head and breast, the white collar and purple wing-patches make him a striking fellow. The brown speckles of the duck make her look tidy, and a little homely, but she flies with equal grace and confidence.

The legend is often revived (by people who do not think very deeply) that all men are equal. But

the animal and bird worlds know better. Leaders are born, and followed. The odd man goes his own way, and the complacent middle men tread their middle path. We had the drake and two ducks. One of the ducks was the leader. She was determined, courageous, and sensible in everything she did. The drake followed her devotedly. Her sister was erratic, unpredictable, nervous and stupid. She flapped around and vacillated, and was treated by the drake as a fussy old bore, though she courted him strongly, bobbing her head and walking backwards and forwards in front of him. She refused to be shut up in an orderly manner with the others when dusk came. (I'm sure you have met someone exactly like this.) I floundered about in the mud on wet nights, and darted after her among the bushes on dry ones, and sometimes had to give up and shut her out, if there was no-one around to help me.

One night the leader was missing. There was no sign of her, and we had to leave it until morning before we began the search. Their run, including the pond, was nearly half an acre, and there was long grass, shrubs and a rough hedge to hide in or under.

We soon found her, sitting on a nest she had made in the long grass. We left her, and waited. Later in the day we saw her swimming on the pond, and we went to examine her nest. We should not have been able to find it had we not marked the place when she was sitting. She had covered it with grass, moss, and down from her breast, so that no egg was visible. We realised that there was a large clutch of eggs, though we did not disturb them to count.

We watched every day to see that she was safe, and she sat as close as a pheasant, her colouring being perfect camouflage. When the incubation period was almost over we set a hencoop over her and wired in a short run to keep her from the attentions of rats.

Imagine our surprise when her family emerged and we counted nineteen little mallards. She had reason to be proud, and when we picked up one to examine it she thrust her head through the slats and banged and pecked at our hands. But she did not rear them all: she was restless and we found several of them trodden on and dead. The mother's instinct to guard her offspring is an automatic reaction, having nothing to do with reason or intelligence. Game-birds will trail their tiny young through impossibly difficult places when they are wet and exhausted; then they fall down and lie until they die or are killed, the mother taking no notice.

Our mallard's instinct for freedom proved strong, and we decided we must let her take them to the pond when she wished. They were a bonny sight, puffs of yellow and brown, rounder than tame ducklings, bobbing on the quiet surface.

They popped under and stood on their heads, they darted after flies immediately they touched the water, and were immensely swift for creatures so small.

Several more died, most likely from exhaustion, and we came to the conclusion that it would have been better to have taken them from their mother at birth and put them in the care of a broody hen for the first period of their lives.

It was a lovely picture: the mother waddling along with a whole army of peeping ducklings, running, gobbling, marching behind her. She passed Game fearlessly but slowly, quietly quacking to her family, encouraging them to appear dignified and calm. Game looked affectionately amused, standing beside me and awaiting my reaction, but when she saw there was none, she sneezed, wagged her tail and sat down.

The fussy sister duck made a nest and laid several eggs, but her brooding was like the rest of her deeds, more off than on. Though fertile, the eggs never hatched.

During the summer the adult ducks and drake used both ponds, sometimes rising straight off the water and flying around with a soft whistling sound to alight again with a splash. The take-off was preceded by a repeated upward thrusting of the head. They grew wilder with such freedom, and occasionally did not return to their tumbril at dusk. But they came back during the day.

It was a hard winter that year. The youngsters were confined to their enclosure. The stream gradually froze. The garden pond became solid ice. The old birds still slept on the field pond, keeping a pool of water in the centre by slightly paddling their feet all night. We tried to coax them home but they ignored persuasion, and one morning the stupid duck had vanished. We found tracks of a fox and thought he must have taken them by surprise by walking over the surface while they slept. Fortunately it was the dizzy one that was missing, and no-one minded. That day, the centre pool of water also froze, and we drove the ducks into the stable each evening. 'Yes, yes, that'll keep Mr Rinkser without a supper,' said Tom.

A few nights after his kill, I think I saw the culprit. I woke about midnight and sat up in bed to look across towards the pond; it was bright moonlight, and the snow added a radiance to the air. It was the right moment, for I saw a large dog-fox sit down about twenty yards from the pond. He remained motionless on the snow. It was an astonishing sight, and I went and woke John, who also watched from his window. The fox still did not move, and after some minutes I put my hands outside the window and clapped them. Still he did not move, though he turned his head as if to listen. This surprised me, so I clapped louder, and he cantered into the shadow of the hedge and disappeared. The next morning we went to find his pad-marks. He had been through the garden, found the duck pen, jumped over the gate, and nosed around the stable door. Snow is a splendid detective.

After that we guarded our mallards carefully, and in the spring Reginald Appleyard, water-fowl breeder, and a great friend, came over, and soon spotted our attractive birds. The youngsters were not as fine as their parents, but it was too early to judge. He asked us to sell him the entire family for breeding. We hesitated. We knew that if Reggie wanted them they must be good indeed. They were beautiful and had become a part of our landscape. The air is never really empty or lonely if at an unexpected moment one can see a flight of sunlit wings rise, and pass, and fall and rise again, breasting the sky for the joy of flying.

But we were shortly to leave the farm, and we should have to part with them then. So, reluctantly, we let them go.

The bonny duck fought when we caught and boxed her. The drake did not mind. But with ducks there is no such thing as caring, or remembering. Freedom, food and water are all they ask – affection is not part of their make-up. Sometimes I think there is a lot to be said for being a wild duck, with bright feathers and powerful wings – the sky is so vast, and the earth so beautiful.

NUTHATCHES

THE OAK TREE was about a hundred years old. Not very old, but old enough. It stood at the corner of one of the rides of our overgrown wood, so it was very tall and not so robust as it might have been had it stood alone in a meadow. We could see it from our windows. About fifteen feet from the ground there was a hole in its side, big enough to have allowed one to slip in a green-gage plum.

We should never have known about the hole except for a pair of nuthatches. They discovered it and decided to build there and hatch a brood of darting, squealing, eager babies. Their call-note is not very attractive, and so monotonous that it never could be called a song, but their tapping, rather like that of a woodpecker, is a friendly noise; it causes one to look up and watch. And they are suavely beautiful in a simply cut suit – steel-blue on top, buff underneath. They are no bigger than a young thrush.

Alas, the owner of the woods came one day with a small hatchet and chopped away a disc of bark at the base of the oak. This meant that the tree was to be felled; the mark was for the foresters to find.

It was March, and one day, when I had been to market in Bury St Edmunds, I came back in the afternoon to find the immense oak (a tree always looks much bigger lying down than standing up) laid so that its higher branch-tips were across the ditch surrounding our lawn, with masses of broken twigs and smaller branches strewn for some distance, as a result of the enormous crash when it fell. I was glad I had not seen it as it swayed and split and thundered down.

It was some days before the men 'tidied it up'. Then they made heaps of its small branches, sawed off the larger ones, and left the trunk clean, slightly raised from the ground by two of its boughs placed cross-wise under it.

Right in the centre of its side was the hole that the nuthatches had started to use before their site was felled so rudely. Obviously it had been a natural knot in the tree, and the tunnel it made was several inches long.

April came, and blackbirds built a nest in the heap of twigs. We saw the nuthatches again busily darting about examining the trees in the neighbourhood. But all the birds do this at the first sign of spring, and we took little notice. We have several nesting-boxes, and these too were being examined by small birds with a view to moving in. We knew better than to pry too closely into their home plans. Time discloses all facts.

The day John went back to school for the summer term, he took a final stroll to see whatever of interest there was before he set off. There was a hole in the bank of the ditch where a vixen was lying, a newly made squirrel-drey in the beech copse, a nightingale singing in the osier bed, and countless blackbirds and thrushes at work. Suddenly: 'Come and look!' I went, and saw the two nuthatches flying in and out of the hole in the felled oak. 'I wonder if you could give them some sort of a roof?'

'A roof?'

'A heavy downpour could drown the babies.'

John had to catch his train, so I went in search of his 'roof'. The old shed produced it. There was a small oblong wooden box: I broke away the bottom and one side, leaving exactly what I wanted. A few small nails held it in place over the hole, and it was still easy for the birds to enter and leave.

I put a notice on the tree – 'BIRDS NESTING. DO NOT TOUCH. THIS MEANS YOU!' – for it was so tempting to passing children. Then I went into the house and hoped for the best. For two days the cock and hen birds flew around angrily chattering and diving, and occasionally settling on the tree to inspect the alteration. On the third day they entered, and continued to line and prepare the nest proper. Before she laid her eggs they had completely stopped up one end of the 'roof' with dried mud, and the entrance facing east was neatly rounded inside, also with mud.

Children came and peeped in and went, respecting the notice. A magpie or two alighted on the great fallen tree and abused the roof they wished was away. A jay or two screamed displeasure. A cock pheasant sat each early morning on the extreme end of the trunk, ignored and ignoring. The little hen nuthatch sat on her eggs until they hatched, and after that spent her day taking in beakfuls of food for her new brood, even as the cock did.

It was almost time for them to fly, and one evening I was sitting at my bedroom window writing, when I heard a blackbird's alarm note, followed by the agitated chattering of many birds. I watched and soon discovered the cause: a weasel was mincing down the ride, quite leisurely, stopping every few feet to look around and sniff the air and the leaves. The little birds dived over him and tried to mob him to drive him away, but weasels are used to such antics, and he took no notice.

He reached the fallen oak, put his forepaws on it, leapt up, leapt down, lifting his muzzle, trying to discover the source of the unaccustomed scent.

He ran farther along the ground in the direction of the nest. He stopped and stood on his hind legs again, raising his muzzle to catch the stronger scent. The parent nuthatches went into a panic. They darted and dived and squealed in a frightening way, but the weasel ignored them. He ran to the end of the log. Nothing there. He ran back, and stopped where the nesting-hole was immediately above him.

This was too much, and I ran downstairs, taking Game with me. She knew my reactions so well that her muscles were taut and her ears pricked before we reached the door. I kept her to heel. I knew that at the first sound of my approach he would vanish, and Game's runnings here and there might send him far afield in fright, only to return later. Weasels are usually far too alert and fast for a dog, disappearing before they are seen.

We walked silently towards the fallen tree. When we were within three yards of it, I spied the weasel, running and sniffing and standing on his hind legs to watch. He had not heard us, perhaps because of the screaming of the birds. When he did he leapt away like a flash, but he was a split second too late – Game had seen him, and I hissed quietly, which to her meant 'Attack!' She shot forward and caught him as he leapt, seizing the back of his neck, lifting him, and smashing him down in one clean thud. He was dead instantly. He exuded his dreadful smell, and Game bit him viciously from end to end. She must have thought him a rat, for she showed a hatred that she never showed to other animals. In rat-hunts with John she had been bitten repeatedly, and the word 'rat' sharpened every sense and turned her blood to quicksilver.

Quiet again, and the nuthatches were safe. Very soon afterwards they flew, four of them, and dived and circled and squealed around their imposing residence before they finally left it for unknown haunts.

Game examined the tree thoroughly each day for quite some time and looked at me for the awaited 'Good lass', which I always gave her. But it was too much of a responsibility, so I removed the roof and blocked the nesting-hole with wood. Weasel-hunting is not a desirable habit, though I admit that that one encounter had something very satisfying about it.

MILLICENT BROCK

FOR YEARS we had had an endless stream of animals and birds to care for. Any injured creature was brought to us to mend and loose, or sometimes to protect until it died. Death is a natural outcome of life, and I knew that, but never found it easy to watch or forget. At the time of which I am writing, we had only a few tame pigeons and two grass-snakes, apart from Game, who was one of us and certainly considered herself one of the staff. So freedom was in sight. 'No more,' I said, 'No more!' No staying in; no getting up at the crack of dawn because a thrush needed worms pushing down its throat every few minutes; no hurrying back with fish for the always-hungry Siamese kittens.

John had just reached the age for a motor-scooter, and had been to Peter Scott's Wild Fowl Trust, Slimbridge, for a fortnight to study wildfowl.

I was expecting him back during the afternoon of this lovely April day, and it was bright and clear, so that nothing would delay him, or cause trouble.

At four o'clock he came, up the lane, and across the turf-bridge into the garden. He usually left his machine in the barn, two hundred yards away. He had a broad smile as he shut off his engine – extra bright, even for a homecoming. He travelled rather like a tinker, with suitcase, parcels, bags and gumboots slung on the frame and handlebars. But in the first few minutes after his arrival, I noticed a small wooden box occupying the safest place, lashed to the carrier and saddle; and this had not been with him when he left home.

I waited. I had an awful suspicion that I was in for another surprise. How many times in the past had it happened – John suddenly producing the oddest animal from somewhere? At such times he always glowed with delight and enthusiasm.

I asked no questions; I should know soon enough. I went into the house and started to make tea; and after unloading, John appeared in the sitting-room doorway, carrying the wooden box. 'Now will you sit down and keep quite still, I've something to show you.' I began to expostulate, 'John—' but got no further. 'Shh, you'll love it. Wait now.' And he proceeded to remove the lid, slipping his hand into the hay the box contained.

He drew it out slowly, and placed on my lap a grey ball of fur, with a wedge-shaped head, and beady eyes set in black and white stripes. A baby badger. 'There. Her name is Millicent.'

One of her front paws was bandaged, but she was lively and not in the least afraid. She was drowsy, because normally she would have been in her sett fast asleep during the day. But she nosed round my knees and arms to explore the suddenly strange surroundings. Then she tried to scratch her way into the dark upholstered corner of the chair seat.

'Don't you love her?' he asked. What could I say? Of course I *did*, because she was alive, and warm, and small, and so alone. But a dozen queries poured into my brain. What *shall* we do with her? What does she feed on? Where will she sleep? How big will she grow (she was smaller than a cat and her teeth were so many white points in her pink gums)? What would Game do about her? And where was my freedom?

John had a solution to all these problems. Do with her? We should bring her up like a puppy – they are wonderful pets. Feed on? Oh, almost anything; she even shared my honey sandwiches when I stopped at the roadside for lunch. She loves goat-milk. Sleep? Oh, in my room. How big? No bigger than a short-legged dog.

Then he told me how he had found her with her paw in a trap the week before, and had taken

her 'home' and doctored her, and fed her on brown bread and milk and porridge. He told me the whole story. We must of course keep her – she was too young to be turned loose again, and she could soon be trained, Mr Scott was delighted with her, and so on . . . and on. So she stayed.

For several days she spent her time jumping in and out of her box; biting the edges; taking suspicious looks at Game; eating and sleeping. At night, she, in her box, was put in John's room. But he soon decided to make her a kennel with a wired-in concrete run for exercise, so that he could have more sleep. She insisted on exploring his room when it was dark, and could not resist the chimney. You would be surprised how much noise a baby badger can make in a hollow chimney at one o'clock in the morning. And then there's the question of the cloud of soot when they shake themselves after the adventure.

One night she climbed up into his bed, and spent the rest of the night curled up at his feet. I really believe that she could have wrapped herself in a parcel and tied the string if the idea had occurred to her. A nocturnal animal is a nocturnal animal, and though when she was young daylight held irresistible adventures and cat-naps had to do, as she grew older heredity was too strong, and she slept soundly during most of the day, waking in earnest at dusk.

Her 'kennel' was built in the corner of the goat-house, a complete structure, but extra dark and sheltered by being inside the larger building. A small door cut in the shed side led into her outdoor pen.

We introduced her gradually to her house, and after a few days she retreated to it of her own volition, but she came out every evening (and sometimes during the day) to play with us and Game. She and Game became the closest friends, and chased each other round the garden or dining-room table until they were both panting for breath. When Millicent was inside her wire enclosure nosing about, during the day, Game would go and lie there, touching the wire, waiting for her friend to make the first move. This was often a sudden attack, grabbing Game by the neck (or ear) and trying to pull her through the large mesh. The bitch's patience was great – she would yelp and wait, trying to ease away, then proceed to lie about a foot away, out of reach, but still keeping a loving eye on the badger.

Game seemed to know that she was playing with an irresponsible baby, and never used her strength to protect herself, as Millicent did. Game would tear round and round an obstacle. Milly would slip over, or under, or through, and cut her off. She had the wild cunning, and never in any way became domesticated, nor did she respond to a command. Where a puppy would be timid about jumping from a height, she had no hesitation in hurling herself into the air. The first time she did, it was frightening: she was sitting quietly on my lap, when she suddenly took a flying leap at Game, missed her, and landed with a sprawl six feet away. She looked astonished, shook herself, and came back none the worse.

We fed her on goat-milk, which John used to fetch every evening from the village, leaving me in charge of two tumbling animals. In her playfulness Millicent would nip my ankles as she ran round the chair legs, and as her teeth grew this ceased to be funny. Badgers are known for their terrifically powerful jaws. Several nights, John returned to find me bunched up on the dining-room table, not daring to get down, with Millie standing on her hind legs nosing the table top for the vanished

ankles and ignoring all commands to 'Go away.' She never learnt what 'No' meant.

She loved a vase of flowers. She sniffed them, then nibbled them, then pulled the whole lot over and ran for her life. One large jar of them always stood in the corner of the sitting-room on the floor to fill a gap. Once she had discovered them, they had to be moved before she came into the house, or the first thing she did was tip them over.

We had an enclosed spiral staircase at each end of the cottage, with a door at the foot of each. Millie mounted the stairs in bounds if she saw that one of the doors had been left open, and literally skipped from room to room upstairs, under the beds, behind the furniture, hiding in dark corners, and generally revelling in her cleverness in having managed to get there before she was discovered and carried down. Hide and seek was natural to her, and when caught she tried a few quick nips, hoping the hands would release her, but when she found that she got a smack on the nose with my flat hand each time she tried it, she soon stopped. A badger would not be a satisfactory ruler of a household, as we had to discover.

As it grew dusk she became more brave and swift in her movements; then we had to keep our wits about us. On the lawn she would weave in and out and round about our legs, and would suddenly go 'bottle-brush' – her hair standing on end, making her look like a tremendous hedgehog in the half-light. She ran swiftly and cantered like a small bear, and her shiny nose burrowed into all holes in the grass or earth. This was followed by swift sharp digging with those two fork-like front paws (both of them by now strong and healed), and one could easily realize how a badger's sett can become so large. Their legs and head are powerfully tough. I have heard it said that a badger's bite can leave marks on an iron spade, and I believe it. A dog that faces a badger fighting for her life stands a chance of being killed by her.

Millicent ate her bread and milk exactly as a pig does, all sucking noise and greed. She would allow no-one to touch her or the bowl until the dish was empty, not even John, whom she loved above all others. Even Game knew better than to approach her dish once it was placed on the ground with

Millie in the vicinity. A badger darts its head as fast as a lizard does, when it wants to bite, and that bite was to be avoided. She gave one's hand a hard knock with her head if she wanted it out of the way.

A careful check was kept on her weight and condition. Every Friday evening she was popped into a sack and hung from a balance. When she was nearing twenty pounds she was too large to be allowed in the house any longer, and had to have her fun in the garden, with John and Game to see that she behaved reasonably. We had a hive of bees, and we never dared to let her know, or she would probably have treated it as she did a vase of flowers – she sucked greedily at a spoonful of honey. Her territory had to be at the other end of the garden, at the edge of the woods.

She often broke away and ran to the back door, unable to understand why she was kept on the outside of such a lovely store, but though a badger does respond to certain training, it never becomes obedient, and its body is lumbering and clumsy, so her indoor frolics were over.

Many people and children visited and handled her. She never tried to bite them. But that was always during the day, when she was slower and a little sleepy, not caring very much what happened. Her hearing was sensitive, and after dusk her ears twitched at the slightest sound, and she charged away at full speed from the direction of the noise. I think perhaps that she would not have allowed a stranger near her at night.

She was a great pet and always amusing; but when she weighed twenty-three pounds, we thought it might be kind to send her to a friend of ours in Essex who had a boar badger with whom she could mate and have companionship and much more freedom. We knew from statistics that the nearest wild badgers were a dozen or more miles away. We sensed that she was growing restless. Several nights she had bitten her way through the wire surrounding her run, though she always returned to her bed at daybreak.

Millicent was now full-grown and very handsome. John had been in touch with the Essex people, and it was left that he should wire them the day he decided to take her down there.

It was early morning of the day of final decision. He had drafted the message he intended to telegraph by phone. He walked out to look if Millie were awake, with mixed feelings: he loved her dearly and hated to see her go.

I was standing at the open window, and suddenly he called to me: 'She's gone!' Together we examined her kennel. She had bitten a hole in the wire as round and large as a dinner plate. The earth outside was dry and hard, so we could not see in what direction she had gone. There was nothing we could do but await her usual return. We left a piece of rabbit in her bed for when she came back.

The day went by, and night came, but no Millie. John attached a cord to a dead rabbit which he left in her pen, delicately fixed and supported the cord, and carried the end through his bedroom window. At his end he hung a light stuffed bird, and it was so fixed that it would fall on his pillow at the slightest tug at the rabbit Millie was bound to make as soon as she returned.

He waited for five days and nights. We thought she might call on us at least once, as this had been her home for so long. But she was at last free, and did not. She may have come during the night and left no trace, but her sleeping-quarters remained untouched. Obviously she was finding enough food in her own way. She was a wild creature in spite of all, and wanted to be off. We knew it was best for her, though we should never have turned her away in case she could not feed herself, having been dependent on us for so long. So she settled her own problem and ours, and went back to the life she was born for.

The Christmas after she broke loose, John was walking in the snow about two miles from home, when he saw the imprint of a badger's paw, unmistakable because so different from any other animal's owing to the long sharp claw-marks and their distance from the five toe-pads. He had not given up the idea that someday he would catch up with her again, so he tried to follow them. They showed for the length of a lane, but melting snow hid further tracks. It proved, however, that Millicent was alive five months after she had left us.

The following spring we were told that the Hunt had seen a badger sett in a wood several miles from us. So off John set one late evening. He found it – the large hole and the trodden pile of earth at its mouth are easily spotted – and hid at the foot of an oak tree, downwind.

When it was quite dark, and after he had heard many wild sounds but none of them the one he was listening for, a familiar shuffle told him that, though he could not see, Millicent was there, within a few feet of him. The sound stopped. He heard her scratch her shoulder with her hind paw, a rough, grating scratch she always indulged in when she first woke, which we had watched and heard, and laughed at, many times.

He was tempted to call her by name, to make some contact, but did not. Perhaps it would have frightened her needlessly. He had found the proof he wanted, and he stayed silent.

After sniffing the air and making a gentle hummering noise she moved away, quite unconscious of the fact that she had delighted a loving eavesdropper by her wild presence and greedily taken independence.

MERLIN

HERE I have to be very careful. Every morning a thrush sings in these woods near enough to wake me. He calls: 'Hesperides, Hesperides, Look! ... Weep Weep ... Hesperides, Hesperides ...' Last year there was one that called: 'Eurydice, Eurydice,' in plaintive French ... oh so sad to hear. That is fact; no-one can accuse me of not hearing correctly. But when I come to write of hawks, my experiences are likely to be examined and analysed. They are birds of prey, another matter. However, this account is of my own observations.

It is natural that one interested in all forms of bird and animal life should develop a study of them; we had kept canaries, finches, a parrot, jackdaws, jays, pigeons, a dove, all kinds of fledglings, and three owls. When John read about eagles and hawks, and articles on falconry, there was only one terminus possible, and he obviously intended to head for it. The discovery that the secretary of the British Falconers' Club lived only twelve miles away flooded his horizon with sun (and flooded my horizon). Hawks? My ignorance concerning them was profound: their 'activities' had been confined to the sight of a sparrow-hawk swooping at terrific speed into the stable yard and taking a flying sparrow very close to my shoulder.

An invitation to 'talk hawks' was accepted with frightening enthusiasm by John, and a road was laid that stretches unendingly into the future. Risby Manor became John's second home, and Major Guy Aylmer the finest friend a boy ever had.

First a kestrel had to be trained, then a sparrow-hawk. I dismiss this in a few words, but actually they were involved undertakings for a novice, and from them John learned certain essential principles. He boarded a peregrine falcon for the Major for some weeks, acting under instruction. But in every case I was something of a culprit. I was accused (though kindly) of either 'creeping' or 'crashing' whenever I put in an appearance. These wild, nervous birds prefer men, I feel sure – men wear sombre clothes that do not blow in the wind, and their movements are slower. They train the birds and each becomes accustomed to the other. Enter a woman in their line of vision, no matter at *what* pace she moves, and it means that the hawk will bate (beat its wings, fall upside down, panic, what you will) until it has become used to her peculiarities (and a woman has no idea how peculiar she is until she meets a strange hawk!). We lived an isolated existence, and for days on end John and I saw only each other. I suspect that, had there been other human beings about, I should have passed unnoticed, and certainly less self-consciously.

When the peregrine first appeared on the block on the lawn, old gamekeeper Josh, passing, saw it and stopped: 'Poll, Poll,' he called.

I went towards him: 'That is a peregrine, Josh.'

'That's a parrot, I reckon. That's an ode parrot. Here, Poll.'

And a parrot it remained to him – nothing could convince him otherwise. The old boy was uneducated, and could neither read nor write, and had never heard of a peregrine. He would stand for long enough, fascinated, watching 'Poll, here Poll.'

After a good deal of experience and actual hawking in Suffolk and Wiltshire, John told me he was expecting a merlin. I prepared for a few extra flutterings in more ways than one.

Oddly enough, it never happened. The merlin arrived from Caithness, two months old, sent by rail in a box with another merlin. There is magic in its name, and there was magic in itself. It was responsive and graceful. (In the golden age of falconry the merlin was the lady's hawk.) Its large eyes were without fear, and it was neat in its postures and actions. She was a little larger than a mistle-thrush. Her upper parts were dark brown, and her breast brown-streaked on a buff ground, with a small cream 'bib'. A dark vertical line from her eyes to her throat gave her a serious look. Her flight was sharp and dashing, though she would glide and swerve and suddenly mount high in the air. John named her Latifa, which is Persian for 'pretty girl'.

John had built a hawk house on to the south side of the goat-shed. The latter provided the main wall. Outwards from this he erected the remaining three sides, of double wire netting packed with a foot of straw to form warm walls. He inset two windows with protective wire inside, sunblinds, and a self-closing door. He added a concrete floor, and capped the whole structure with a steep-sloping corrugated-iron roof, and fenced in an adjoining plot of grass. He furnished the inside of the house with several horizontal branches, brackets, and a screen-perch (a bar from which hung weighted sacking), and the floor he covered with sawdust. It was warm, rain-proof and light, the most ingenious of all the erections that went up in the name of necessity. (I quite imagined the day might dawn when I should be asked to vacate the house for John's hawks, and use their shed, but it did not.)

The evening the merlin arrived John carried her indoors to have her jesses fastened to her legs.

Jesses are soft leather thongs, one for each leg, which are attached to a leash by a small metal swivel. By this means she could be secured to a hawk-block without in any way being restricted in movement. A brass hawk-bell, no bigger than a pea, and light as air, was fastened to one foot by that ingenious manipulation of leather practised by falconers. We wrapped her in a large silk kerchief while this operation was being carried out, to save her from spoiling her plumage by struggling. That over, she was taken to her house and fed. Merlins live on small birds. When in captivity, bits of raw rabbit and rodent have to supplement their diet.

John sat beside her, quite quiet, for upwards of an hour, and then very gently offered her some pieces of raw meat on the tips of his fingers. She pecked him, and so took some of the meat in her beak, and swallowed it. But it took another hour before she had had sufficient for the night.

He spent most of the next day sitting with her, getting her used to his presence and giving her confidence. He slowly touched her feet and breast, and talked softly to her. A hawk is always held on a gloved fist, and he put on this gauntlet and offered her food. It took much tact to get her to accept it, but knowledge and sufficient patience overcame most obstacles.

For several days after that he took her on his fist into the woods and fields, walking with her for

hours, getting her used to the sights and sounds, and the few people around. He fed her at the fist and she relaxed and took the sparrows and pulled them apart with her beak as she would have done in the wild. At John's approach she stood on tiptoe and wafted her wings. She took a great delight in her daily bath. She walked busily round the edge, dipping her beak, rousing, waiting, and glancing to see that she was undisturbed. After these preliminaries, which sometimes lasted for ten minutes, she stepped in gingerly, and dipped her face, shuffling her wings and so splashing the water over herself. She looked strangely defence-less with her wet spikey feathers, and not until she had dried herself, by shaking, rousing and preening, did she regain her look of immense dignity and repose.

Half the art of manning is to keep the birds from over-domestication. They must be compliant and confident but at the same time retain their wild propensities. Training can be accomplished in ten days. John made a lure. This was a small oblong biscuit of lead, padded (like a pin-cushion), and encased in scarlet felt. To it, he sewed up two sparrow-wings. Lures are attached to a long string and thrown down on the ground after being whirled round the head several times. The watching hawk, thinking it a small flying bird, swoops on to it and holds it, and together they are lifted by the trainer, who substitutes a piece of meat for the lure, which he then slides from under the hawk's claws. (During this training, the hawk is also attached to a creance (long cord) secured to its jesses, until such time as it can be trusted to fly free and return to the fist.)

I remember the first time that Latifa was brought on to the lawn to be tried out. The stem of a wooden T-shaped perch was pushed into the ground, and John placed her on the horizontal top. A creance about twenty feet long was attached to her jesses. It was light, and could not impede her flight, but would hold her if she made an attempt to fly away. He swung the lure in a circle several times, and then released it. She watched, made as if to fly after it, ruffled her feathers, moved from foot to foot, then shook herself and settled down again. He repeated the movements, Latifa watching keenly. Still she hesitated. He swung it again, round and round and round, and down, and she flew straight on to it, and held it with her claws. He approached slowly and cautiously, and slid a tempting piece of raw meat held in his gloved hand, under her feet. She relaxed, and accepted it, and he lifted her up. She was allowed several mouthfuls, and then restored to the T-perch to go through the same exercises again. John beamed success.

This continued for several days, and in between training periods she either was carried on John's fist or sat on her block on the lawn, occasionally beating her wings, or walking the length of her leash. Her manners improved rapidly. She ceased to chitter when he approached, and jumped on to his hand voluntarily, without any inducement.

At the end of her ten-day training period, she was released from the creance and put through similar practice. It is always a risk, once the birds are flying loose, but it has to be taken, and it is a great thrill when they return to the lure and respond to one's expectations. Once, in those earliest days she veered off, circled, dipped, circled again, and came to rest on the highest branch of an oak tree beyond the lawn. I hated that moment. I willed her to come down. I wished desperately that she would, and I knew she wouldn't. In fact, I was completely stupid to feel any concern whatsoever. I could not turn the scale because I was indoors looking through the window, and John was doing the right things, composed as usual, unconscious of the turmoil invading the onlooker behind the glass.

He was holding her attention by walking about, talking to her and swinging the lure. If he could interest her sufficiently, she would swoop, and fasten her claws on it as she had been taught.

For a long time she was not in the least interested. She preened, moved a few steps further along the branch, shook herself, and settled down to enjoy the new view and freedom. John's eyes dared not leave her. Finally, he fastened a piece of raw sparrow to the lure and swung it in the air again in every direction until she watched. Then he let it fall and dragged it jerkily along the grass. Over and over again. Latifa could not resist this for ever, and by now half an hour had passed.

To be successful, a rider must be one thought ahead of his horse, always, and this is equally true of a boy and his hawk. His eyes were still on her, and he approached nearer to the tree, swung the lure in circles above his head, let it fall, and jerked it until she prepared to fly. Over and over again he did it, watching her, till suddenly, down, as straight as hail, she flew, and fastened on to it. But she was still free, and the slightest error could send her off again.

She had started to eat the sparrow-flesh, and John went down on all fours and crept slowly towards her, talking softly all the time. I held my breath. When almost within reach, he lay full length on the grass, and by inches reached towards her with his arm. Infinitely slowly his fingers approached till they touched her jesses, and she was secure. At least one sigh of relief went up, and John smiled broadly as he carried her back.

That was enough for one day, and she was returned to her block and fed until her gorge bulged sufficiently but not too much. Over-feeding can produce indifference and laziness.

That was her only lapse from grace, and she was flown constantly during that summer. She was taken long distances in an especially prepared box, which was fastened to John's motor-cycle. It contained a perch, and was large enough to allow her to stretch her wings and her tail without their touching the sides and damaging her feathers. She seemed to like travelling, and did not mind the noise and vibration. She emerged as composed as she entered, and was quite ready to re-enter her box when her fun was over for the evening. She watched every step of the proceedings – one felt she was ready to drop a hint or two in the event of difficulties arising.

September came, and John had to be away all that autumn and winter, so he decided to give her her freedom once he was assured that she could, and did, feed herself easily. Guy Aylmer and John were going to Wiltshire for two weeks' hawking on the Downs, so Latifa travelled her final journey in the boot of an old Daimler especially equipped to carry a number of hawks hooded and standing on their padded cadge. Had she been turned back to the wilds here, doubtless she would have been shot by a gamekeeper.

One morning, near Avebury, John turned her loose without jesses or bell. And we have this entry in his diary:

September 30th, . . . Avebury, Wiltshire.
I went out with a lure for Latifa this evening, but there was no sign of her.

117

October 1st . . .

The Major from his bedroom window this morning noticed daws mobbing something on a chimney-stack opposite. It then moved off, and he saw it was Latifa. I finished dressing, in a hurry, and went out with the lure. After some time she came in to the lure on top of the bank, from the direction of the tumulus near where I released her. She was very hungry and her breast bone felt sharp, but a small bird's feather was sticking to one of her legs and she muted normally, so she must have killed. I brought her back to the mews. We fitted a pair of jesses on her while she fed. Went to lunch and tea with S.F., and after giving Latifa a good gorge this afternoon, and removing her jesses again, I turned her out on the edge of Olga's wood. S. will keep an eye open for her, and she probably stands more chance of killing in that sort of country than in down-land. She soared away down wind towards Black Cover.

She was not seen again. She had found her freedom and accepted it in graceful departure.

That ends my account of the merlin, but I think you will find it interesting if I tell you of some very old English phrases which came to be used in falconry, and which have become household phrases for us today. For instance, we sometimes say we are 'fed up', which sounds like sheer slang; but it is a hawking term. When a hawk is fully fed, she is not interested in anything until her food is digested – in other words she is fed up.

'Beating round the bush' is frequently used by us, meaning that we are failing to come directly to the point. The hawk beats round the bush where its quarry has put in.

'Let fly' or lose (loose) our temper. It is the falconer's phrase when he lets his hawk fly at quarry.

'Feather in his cap' is an honour or promotion. A heron was a good capture in the olden days, and the falconer cut a feather from the heron's crest when his hawk caught him, then let the heron go. It was proof of the hawk's skill.

'Crabby' describes bad-tempered people. Two hawks quarrelling are said to 'crab'.

To 'hoodwink' anyone is to try to deceive them. A hawk is hood-winked by having his leather hood put on, to baffle him, and keep him in the dark.

There are many more, handed down for hundreds of years, and used by people who have no idea that they are hawking terms that were used by Henry VIII when he pursued his favourite sport. He did, you know.

BOYS – 1

WE HAD A close friend named Harry
Carstairs, a patient, middle-aged man who
delighted in telling John of his pranks on his
grandfather's estate near Manchester fifty years
before. He told an enthralled nine-year-old how
he had caught and killed hedgehogs, wrapped
them in clay and roasted them on a wood fire. The
theory was that, when they were cooked, the clay
was knocked away, carrying with it the spines, to
reveal a succulent joint. Another ruse was to glue
dried peas to the floor-piece of a steel spring-trap
so that when a pheasant pecked a pea, the jaws of
the trap were sprung, and the pheasant's death
was instantaneous from a broken neck. It, too, was
wrapped in clay and roasted, its feathers coming
away like the hedgehog's spines.

When an elderly man is recalling his boyhood,
his thoughts often become highly coloured, and
perhaps a touch of magic shows itself that was
never there all those years ago ... and 'things
were different then'. Harry told of his exploits

(with relish) and he was a kind and lovable man, whose words John cherished. There is a saying that Jack is as good as his master, and that can surely mean one of two things: perhaps we can tell which, later on.

John's cousin Tommy, a year his junior, spent his holidays with us at the farmhouse and later at the cottage. Busy the day's length and always in summer mood, they were as suited to one another as two leaves on a stalk. Weather made no difference – they were planning or making or collecting; or writing their daily doings in home-made diaries; drawing maps of the woods and meadows, renaming them if plans demanded it; reading, consulting textbooks.

During that summer, we had staying with us a boy, Martin, whose father's farm in the neigh-bouring village had been gutted by fire. He was with us for a few weeks while his parents sorted out the future.

In the rough orchard they started to dig an underground den. This took a considerable time, and a few hands gave assistance, but eventually it was big enough to house three boys and there was a chimney-hole above a dug-out fire-well, where they burned kindling and almost smoke-dried themselves. Several lengths of sturdy wood acted as pit-props, and, recalling it as I do now, my guess is that it was in fairly heavy clay soil. I was invited into it twice, which was quite something, the entrance calling for dexterity in lowering oneself through the fairly slim funnel.

Rationing was still in force then, and food, particularly meat, was not too plentiful. It was a problem for any responsible cook to have enough of any one joint at any one time.

One lovely morning, I was preparing a hit-or-miss dish for our midday meal, and the three boys were in and out of and around their den, much as usual. Suddenly, the kitchen door opened and let in a burst of sunlight and bright-faced Martin: 'Mrs Savidge, how do you thicken gravy?'

I was so surprised that I looked at him and stupidly repeated 'Gravy?' Then the penny dropped: '*Gravy?*'

'Yes, how do you thicken it, please? John wants to know.'

'But where have you got your gravy from?'

'It's a secret,' John said, 'but we shall bring you some, and we shan't want any lunch.'

I know when I am beaten, so I tried to explain gravy-thickening, supplied the necessary ingredients, and crossed my mental fingers. I also went ahead with the normal routine; in health, boys' appetites are fairly constant, I have found.

Eventually, Tommy fetched plates and returned to their den. Not long after, Martin brought me what looked like a piece of pink flannel floating in rain-water. He told me that stewed blackberries would follow, and hoped I should enjoy the feast.

John was 'finishing it off' and carving. I could well believe that. It was roast pheasant à la Carstairs, but the only taste was smoke.

I waited a little while before returning the call, then, with as much tact as I could muster, stated the do's and the do not's. It was the only time that John had turned poacher and chef, and it was to be the last. But it was only common sense to make the best of the pheasant, and I finished the cooking process in my oven, and the boys seemed to think it was not unpleasant.

No day was long enough to see all they knew was there, so one day, John and Tommy (Martin had gone home) decided that if they sat up a tree all night, they would see amazing happenings by moonlight. They went in search of an accommodating tree in a suitable part of the wood, and, having found it, came back to plan and collect their gear. Enormous possibilities were discussed and eventualities allowed for. I agreed with everything, believing it better to travel hopefully than to arrive.

After supper, they were both swaddled in warm clothes, and with packed sandwiches and a Thermos they set off with rugs and great expectations. I promised to leave a door unlocked so that they could enter the house at the earliest sign of dawn.

I went to bed, and after my usual read turned off the light, glancing at the bright moonlight and wishing they were in bed, though in fact they were but a few hundred yards away.

About midnight, I heard quiet creakings and whisperings below, and knew that all was well – they were home. Several hours in a cramped position can be terribly long, and though they had heard rustlings in the leaves, and many noises that woods do make on summer nights, nothing could be seen to hold their heavy-eyed interest and keep them awake. The food and drink had been consumed, boys are forever hungry out of doors, and up a hard oak tree in the darkness, eating is a necessary occupation. Their warm beds had pulled, and back they plodded, happy that they had done it 'to see'. They considered that 'there might have been something later on if we could have waited', and of course, they were right. Life is like that. But there were no regrets about the exploit.

The next day was no more successful. They set out in caps, coats and gumboots – the weather had broken soon after dawn. They came back with broad grins an hour and a half after leaving the house. They dropped a large fisherman-type net in the yard, came in and shut the door behind them without looking back, and exploded with laughs.

They told me that as they walked down the long meadow, with the net under one arm and John's pet ferret curled up in his pocket, they felt someone was behind them, turned round, and saw it was Tobias Cocksedge, Sir John's gamekeeper (Sir John Agnew owned Freewood estate), a sharp old man not noted for friendly conversation.

They slowed down, to let him overtake them, but so did he. Eventually they stopped and he had no option but to catch up with them.

'Where are you going with that net, then?'

'To put it over the peas,'

'*Peas?*'

'Yes.'

'Hmmm . . . on you go then.' The old dodger was a jump ahead of them. He thought.

They had no alternative but to start walking again. When they were out of earshot, though they knew that Cocksedge was still tailing them, they decided to take him for a few miles round the estate. This they did, finally ending up in their own kitchen.

'Tommy wants to take a baby rabbit back with him, and we'd got permission, you know that!'

'But why didn't you tell him to go away? What about the pea story?'

'Tom (your farm friend) told me to settle him if he ever interfered – "Tell 'im it's for the peas" – so I did. Tom always knows what to say.' Actually, he did.

The old man must have been hopping mad, but he had no case. He started something he had to

126

finish. The baby rabbit was caught (and duly turned into a pet) another day.

Shortly after this episode, John's ferret bore a litter of six pure-white babies, and died within twenty-four hours. We were sadder than one would have thought possible over such a happening. She was a tame and gentle creature to handle, but quick as a whiplash in action, and it was hard to reconcile this collapse with her short, healthy life. I suppose that in the country it is brought to our notice more clearly than in the town that for every summer there is a winter, and for every birth a death. We learn that life is the acceptance of both.

Boys – 2

THE WAR had ended, but food was still strictly rationed. Apart from bull-terrier puppies and Siamese kittens we had no strange animals as guests at this particular time. One day, John asked if I would have a boy to stay for two weeks 'from somewhere in Holland'. Children from once-occupied Europe were coming to England for a holiday, and it had been announced at Culford School that parents would be doing a service by housing and entertaining one of them.

I agreed willingly, and felt what a splendid idea it all was. I merely stipulated that it must be a boy, for obvious reasons.

There were several weeks to go before they were due in England, and we began to put on one side rationed fruit, sweets and, towards the latter part of the time, new-laid eggs, which were very scarce. 'Poor children, their lives must have been quite awful – we'll be extra kind, John, and do what we can to help him to forget it all,' and such

admonishments at intervals, but constantly, until the day of his arrival.

I talked to Tom and got his co-operation; he had no children of his own and always took an interest in boys who loved the outdoors. 'He'll be all right, so long as that's not rafty old weather'.

The parents involved were asked to collect their guests from school at 4 o'clock one afternoon in August. I had recently sold our car, and a retired Indian Army Colonel who was a close friend offered to take us over in his Morris Tourer: it would have been quite at home in the London-to-Brighton Old Crocks' Parade. But it was spacious enough, and the hood was permanently down, enabling passengers to see the countryside (if cross-draughts, dust, sun and blown hair allowed them to see anything at all). The foreign child would think it funny, and surely enjoy such a venture after six years of enemy restrictions.

We arrived, with many other parents, and perhaps thirty to forty boys and girls were assembled in the main hall. Members of the staff were introducing them to their respective hosts. From behind where we were standing a master said, 'And now Lane, this is your hostess, Mrs Savidge.' I turned, and saw our young friend who stepped forward, and with military precision shook hands with me and said his one word of greeting: 'Goodbye!' That about summed up his knowledge of English. I tried not to laugh, and it was easy to restrain myself because my mind was racing with surprise. He was five foot ten, splendidly built, beautifully clothed in elegantly cut tweeds, with sleek yellow hair and polished shoes. His suitcase was new, and the largest I had ever seen.

Somehow we loaded the old car, and drove the ten miles home, with sporadic shouted conversation, and, speaking personally, a sinking heart.

John looked thin and pinched and practically in rags beside this Adonis – clothes coupons had not allowed for much but school uniforms.

Lane spent the evening seeing our home, and unpacking – immaculate shirts, hand-knitted stockings, more tweed jackets and knickerbockers.

I thought I must be tactful and find a meeting-ground: 'Do you like music?'

'Ah, jah.' What a relief: there was something then that we could share and discuss. 'Music' can mean many things, though, and we soon found ourselves tuned in to a continental station that blared 'pop' tunes non-stop for at least twelve hours a day.

The next morning we took him to meet Tom and the farm in general. Tom's face was a poem: they could not converse, because Lane's English was negligible, and Tom's was pure Suffolk. In any case Tom seemed speechless. When he saw me alone later in the day, he said, 'I thought you told me he were a poor little old boy, Ma'am. Oh dear oh dear, he's a well-kept thatching-ladder.'

It must have been the longest fortnight I ever spent in my life. We tried to teach him English, while he tried to teach us Dutch, and we usually conversed in poor French, and tried to get to know each other.

He told me that his father was a garage proprietor in Amsterdam, and did a lot of black-market trade with South Americans: hence his clothes. There had been little shortage of food for his family for the same reason. I asked him how he spent his leisure at home. 'Icegold's Dance Saloon.'

132

The quiet farm atmosphere bored him to tears, and he disliked soiling his hands or shoes. He spent most of his mornings talking to me in the kitchen while I cooked. He borrowed a bicycle and rode into Bury St Edmunds to meet his friends and go to the cinema with them. And occasionally he picked his way through the stack-yard and nodded to Tom.

I knew the boredom he was feeling and was sad about it, but I was helpless: nothing that we had to offer him was suitable, and it was useless to go to the goat-shed for a solution this time! He was the only one of his kind in that entire group of visiting children. For the first time ever, I was stumped by a boy.

It is an extraordinary fact that with a strange animal there is always a means of lowering the barrier: they do not speak our language either and there is no communication, but trust can be established very quickly and understanding travels both ways. If there is a barrier between human beings, it is infinitely harder to surmount; it can be so subtle. Love is the answer for all animals, but love means different things to different people, and is not always understood.

After what seemed years, the day of Lane's departure came, and we took him into Bury and waved goodbye.

Weeks afterwards, I received a letter of thanks from his mother, and then a carton of green grapes and an enormous box of chocolates. It was most kind of her, but I still wonder what Lane thought about all of us!

THE TOUSLED
KNOT

So MANY memories have become a tousled
knot impossible to sort out in sufficient detail
to give an accurate account of what happened: the
partridge chicks like fluffy corks, squeezing themselves flat on to a macadam road, hoping to be
invisible; the fourteen plovers on the fells that
mobbed me because I walked too near their nests;
the greenfinches, flycatchers, starlings, yellow-
hammers, that have from time to time needed a
refuge, to live or die; the guinea-pigs and rabbits
of the earliest days; the parentless wild rabbits we
reared on milk given to them from a glass pipette;
the hedgehogs, and toads, and the woodmouse
that led us such a dance.

And there was Molly, John's pony, who loved
the snow, and when it was thick on the ground
pawed it and snorted into it, and, watching our
windows, trumpeted and hummered to us to go
out and play with her. If we did, she galloped to

us, and pulled our sleeves, shook and tossed her head and galloped round the meadow, and bucked, kicking the snow high into the air with her hind hoofs. Half Welsh, half Arab, bright chestnut with black mane and tail, she was never hogged or docked and her beauty remained as bright as a summer day.

There was the herd of heifers, who used to stand at the gate and watch inquisitively whatever we did; and one by one put out their tongues to lick the outstretched hand and blow it with their sweet, warm breath.

There was the cuckoo that liked our garden, sat on the fence, using his tail as an oar each time he *cuckoo*-ed, and when he flew away was chased by small birds which he ignored; and then the two cuckoos flying together above us, making a bubbling noise like the suppressed gobble of a turkey. And one autumn a white barn owl skimming the lawn and wafting leisurely up one of the woodland rides, every early afternoon for weeks.

A fearless wren and the nest (in the thatched roof of our coal house) we had to rebuild three times deserve remembering. The nest housed her four chicks, and rats destroyed it. The fall must have saved their lives, and ultimately we had to sling them in their patched-up nest in a wire hammock from the roof, to keep them from further attack. Throughout it all the wren never deserted her chicks, and she launched three successfully. John and Tommy hid themselves one day, and made a written record of the number of times she visited the nest with food in her beak. It averaged once in every minute and a half throughout the day, from dawn to dusk.

We recovered young thrushes who had fallen to earth prematurely, owing to the precarious position and the inadequate size of their nest. We put the whole outfit into a cardboard box and tied them to a tree, and watched the mother bird return and continue to feed them through wire netting we placed over the top temporarily.

Few springs can have passed without numerous misfortunes and rescues, and we have had to learn not to mind too much when there is nothing we can do. Pity is not enough. One must know what a creature needs. Sometimes killing is the least cruel way (though one I am usually too much of a coward to take). Once, when John was out to shoot a rabbit to feed his hawks, he saw in the brown bracken a movement which he thought was a rabbit. He fired, and to his grief saw that he had hit a fox, but without killing it. He ran to it and found it badly injured, and had to kill it outright with a second shot. He came back pale and shaken, in tears. The decision to fire that second shot was the worst decision he had ever had to take.

So if after reading these stories you think you must possess one of the animal subjects, be quite sure before you do that you know all that it involves in the way of care, attention and knowledge. There are two VIPs involved, and you are the lesser. Think about it very carefully, and if there are any doubts, decide *not* to. Remember that I had them without the asking, but had reared three human little animals of my own.

One can have a place in the lives of untamed animals and birds without owning them. Actually, they are more interesting in their wild habitat, free of fear and a restricting environment. But one thing is essential: learn to be still, and to watch and observe. Walking down a country lane swishing the grasses with a stick is not likely to produce results. Everything will cower until the disturbance is over.

Yesterday I was walking alone down one of the rides towards the cottage. A hare cantered towards me, in the centre of the path, ears pricked, eyes wide open. We got to within a few yards of each other and I purposely waved a hand to warn him. He turned at right angles into the bracken, but only at lolloping speed. He was not in the least concerned. They are curious creatures, rather stupid, not nearly so wily as rabbits – a rabbit would have scuttled away and leapt to safety at the first sound of an approach.

Then a red squirrel bounded across the path and ran up the trunk of an oak tree. He had a twig in his mouth, with two hazelnuts and a leaf

attached to it. At about seven feet from the ground he paused to watch me, but he made no sound, nor did he drop his twig. He ran up, and round, and out of sight.

I had passed a wood-mouse making a tunnel under the dried leaves, and I was able to watch him for minutes, since he had no idea of my presence.

So if you would really *see*, go alone, go quietly, and keep your eyes wide open.

AFTERTHOUGHT

JOHN SAVIDGE became a game warden in Africa and his life with wild animals has been recounted by Colin Willock in *The Enormous Zoo*. Many boys have asked me, 'How do you become a game warden?' I do not know a short answer, nor even a long one. Love of birds and animals is innate, like many other loves; and if we want anything enough, we shall do all we can to achieve it. Success is not always at the end of the endeavour, but when it is, it rests on a sure foundation and is likely to endure.

These memories of mine deal with John's years from nine to sixteen; but I cannot remember a time, after he had learnt to talk, when his mind was not filled with thoughts of birds, beasts, reptiles, in fact any living creature.

The exercise books he used at school are splashed with sketches of ridiculous little animals, of wild animals being stalked by little men with their hair standing on end, and of horses, deer, elephants.

He had great good fortune in his home, his friends, his school and college, and the fact that he was free to follow where his treasure led; but also, he pursued his uneasy course through the essential stages of preparation, and without that his dreams would still have been curling upwards in pipe-smoke.

But for the Nightingale

Sigh me the many pleasured sighs,
Let poets' praise of every flower
And herb and loaded pippin-bower
Outsound the rooks in winter skies.

Though summer sees the poppy blaze,
And early primrose wakes the weald,
Though nights be ever sable-sealed
And morning veils the sapphire days,

Forget-me-not is scorpion-grass
And I have seen my summers fall
Where owls glide and the vixens call
And few men to their labour pass;
And heard the bats that flap and strain
Under the thatch at breaking-light,
And rats that scratch th' unquiet night,
To strip the loaded summer grain.

Drought robs the wells; and ditches flood;
Fire logs are sealed in bitter mould,
Frail fingers mutiny with cold,
Wind bayonets the thinning blood.

Yet . . . when the April night-bird sings,
Stabs the stale wits with gold and myrrh
And flaunts his poniard-song for her,
My heart out-soars all mortal things.

Mary Denyer